f BRISTOL.

GEOGRAPHIA.

# BATH AND BRISTOL,

## WITH THE COUNTIES OF

SOMERSET AND GLOUCESTER.

DISPLAYED

IN

# A SERIES OF VIEWS;

INCLUDING THE

## MODERN IMPROVEMENTS, PICTURESQUE SCENERY,

### Antiquities, &c.

FROM ORIGINAL DRAWINGS

BY

## THOS H. SHEPHERD,

WITH

### Historical and Descriptive Illustrations

## BY JOHN BRITTON, ESQ: F.S.A.&c.

Drawn by Tho. H. Shepherd.  Engraved by W. Tombleson.

ENTRANCE TO BATH, FROM THE BRISTOL ROAD.

LONDON,

PUBLISHED BY JONES & Co. TEMPLE OF THE MUSES, FINSBURY SQUARE.

APRIL 4, 1829.

Published 1969

© 900409 93 2

*Published by Frank Graham, 6 Queen's Terrace*
*Newcastle upon Tyne 2*

*Printed in Great Britain by Fletcher & Son Ltd, Norwich*
*Bound by Richard Clay (The Chaucer Press) Ltd, Bungay, Suffolk*

# BATH AND BRISTOL,

WITH THE COUNTIES OF

## SOMERSET AND GLOUCESTER,

DISPLAYED IN

### 𝔄 𝔖𝔢𝔯𝔦𝔢𝔰 𝔬𝔣 𝔙𝔦𝔢𝔴𝔰;

INCLUDING THE

MODERN IMPROVEMENTS, PICTURESQUE SCENERY, ANTIQUITIES, &c.

*FROM ORIGINAL DRAWINGS,*

BY THOS. H. SHEPHERD;

WITH HISTORICAL AND DESCRIPTIVE ILLUSTRATIONS,

BY JOHN BRITTON, F.S.A. M.R.S.L.

AND MEMBER OF SEVERAL OTHER ENGLISH AND FOREIGN SOCIETIES.

CRESCENT, BATH.

LONDON:

PUBLISHED BY JONES AND COMPANY,
TEMPLE OF THE MUSES, (LATE LACKINGTON'S,) FINSBURY SQUARE.
1829.
[ENTERED AT STATIONERS' HALL.]

## THE LORD BISHOP OF BATH AND WELLS,

*&c. &c.*

MY LORD,

    IN addressing a Topographical Work on Somersetshire to your Lordship, I appeal to one who is familiar with the whole district, and who can fully appreciate a literary and graphic publication, which professes to contain faithful representations and accounts of the Scenery, Antiquities, and modern Beauties, of that interesting County. It is proper to apprise your Lordship, that whilst our Engravings will aim at the popular province of giving pleasing and correct Views of the fine Buildings, the venerable Ruins, and the picturesque Scenery of the County, our literary matter will be dictated by a scrupulous regard to truth, and a solicitude to amuse as well as to inform the general reader; and that although the price of the publication is so very moderate, still, no exertions or expense will be spared, to render it at once worthy of the subject, and of that extensive patronage which the publishers have already experienced in similar Works, brought out on the same principle —that of combining excellence with cheapness, and trusting to a liberal and discerning public for remuneration, through the means of a widely extended circulation.

That topographical writing is susceptible of being rendered at once entertaining and interesting, will be readily admitted by those who have studied the works of a Pennant, a Warton, a Whittaker, a Hunter, and a Scott. To emulate such distinguished and honoured examples, will ever be the zealous endeavour of one who has much pleasure in subscribing himself

YOUR LORDSHIP'S

Obliged and obedient Servant,

JOHN BRITTON.

LONDON, JULY 1, 1829.

# TOPOGRAPHICAL CHARACTERISTICS

OF THE CITIES OF

# BATH AND BRISTOL,

### DISPLAYED IN A SERIES OF ENGRAVED VIEWS OF THE SCENERY AND BUILDINGS, AND BY DESCRIPTIVE ACCOUNTS OF THOSE CITIES.

---

## CHAPTER I.

#### BATH AND BRISTOL COMPARED.—BRIEF HISTORY OF BATH.

THE accompanying Illustrations of the natural scenery and artificial objects of BATH and BRISTOL, will furnish the stranger with decided information respecting the exterior forms of buildings, their peculiar positions, and the aspect of the diversified landscape on which they are built, and by which they are surrounded.

These Cities, though within thirteen miles of each other, have scarcely one feature or characteristic trait of resemblance. They are as unlike, in edifices, inhabitants, and contiguous scenery, as if belonging to different nations, and a different race of people. Whilst the Bristolians seem to live only to get and save money, the Bathonians are daily occupied in spending it. Both, however, are seeking their respective pleasures : habit and custom tend to reconcile mankind to the sphere in which they move, and the pursuits in which they are engaged. Idleness, to the person of industrious habits, would be as irksome and miserable, as hard labour to the sauntering dandy.

*Bath* exhibits a series of handsome houses with free-stone fronts, covered by stone tiling, and ornamented with all the five orders, as well as many fancies, of architecture— whilst the streets are wide, the inhabitants gay, devoted to pleasure and amusements ; and the surrounding scenery, though hilly and abrupt, is covered with fine turf, woods, and varied plantations. The substratum is alike contra-distinguished from that of Bristol; being an endless bed of fine, soft, but durable free-stone.

We may briefly characterize *Bristol,* as being an active, busy port: having its river and docks crowded with trading vessels, its streets narrow, and the houses consisting of all sorts of materials—timber, plaster, brick, stone, &c. The inhabitants are mostly engaged in commerce, trade, and manufactures. They are diligently and sedulously employed in administering to the luxuries and wants of the more wealthy classes of society: but at the same time laying by a provision for their own future comforts. The surface of the earth, and its substrata, are alike dissimilar to those of the neighbouring City.—Here, as at Bath, the hills are steep and abrupt, interspersed with narrow valleys, and some of them clothed with an almost ever-green verdure, and adorned with fine woods: but they are also craggy, broken, and abound with wild precipices. Hard limestone rocks, of fine marble, prevail to the north and west of the City, whilst a red sand-stone is found to the east and south-east. These characteristic features and varieties of natural and artificial objects, we shall have occasion to display and describe in the progress of the present work.

## BATH.

### BRIEF ACCOUNT OF ITS GENERAL HISTORY.

Without paying much respect to the fabled story of Bladud and his pigs; to the reputed scrofulous or leprous disorders which were eradicated by the Bath waters; or to the disputable origin of the City under the names of *Caer badon, Caer bladin, Caer cran,* or *Caer yn nant Twymin,* we proceed at once to a period when we may more successfully endeavour to rescue truth from the meretricious trammels of fiction, and substitute for the unstable foundations of romance, the firm basis of history.

It is generally allowed that the district, in which Bath is situated, was colonized by a tribe of the *Belgæ,* or *Ædui* of Lower Burgundy, about two hundred and fifty years before the advent of Christ; and that two centuries afterwards, they were reinforced by another horde of continental adventurers, denominated *Cangi.* These barbarous tribes, who had probably discovered the medicinal virtues of the waters, are supposed to have established their principal residence on this sequestered spot; which, in compliment to *Sol,* their chief deity, they called *Solmerton,* "the sun-pool-town." Although this conjecture may be deemed hypothetical, it is in some degree strengthened by the similar signification of the known Roman names given to Bath: *Aquæ Solis,* "waters of the sun;" and *Fontes Calidi,* "hot springs."

The western part of England, and especially Somersetshire, is said to have been subdued by Claudius, the lieutenant of Vespasian, the Roman general; and as we have indubitable proof that his troops were for a considerable time in the neighbourhood of Bath, it may fairly be concluded that the town was enlarged, if not originally built, under the direction of him, or of his more immediate successors. That the healing virtues of its springs were known to the Romans, is evident from the architectural remains of baths, temples, and other edifices of that people, which have been discovered on the site of modern Bath, at various times; and we are well assured, that early in the third century, the waters of this place were by them solemnly dedicated to Apollo Medicus, to whose honour a bronze statue was erected.

After the expulsion of the Roman legions, *Aquæ Solis* appears to have remained in comparative tranquillity for several years: but during the bloody and protracted wars between the Southern Britons and the Saxons, it was the theatre of many obstinately contested conflicts. About the end of the fifth, and beginning of the sixth centuries, the Saxon generals, Ælla and Cerdic, were successively defeated here by the renowned Prince Arthur: in 557, the town was besieged and taken by the Saxon leaders, Ceaulin and Cuthwin. While under their sway, its name was changed from *Aquæ Solis*, to *Hat-Bathun;* "Hot-Baths," and *Acemannes cester*, or "the sick man's city." By these appellations and their derivatives, *Balnea, Badonia, Badonessa, Bathonia, Acamannus,* and *Achumanens,* it is subsequently designated by the Saxon and monkish chroniclers. In the sixth century, its inhabitants were converted to Christianity, and a temple, which had previously been dedicated to Minerva, is said to have been converted into a Christian church. In succeeding ages, other religious houses were founded here by the West Saxon kings. A Nunnery was commenced in 676, which was destroyed by the Danes, and rebuilt by king Offa, about 775, and this was honoured by bequests and grants from different monarchs. Athelstan increased the importance of the town by the establishment of a Mint, and, like many of his successors, both Saxons and Danes, made it a place of temporary residence.

Early in the tenth century the Nunnery was changed to an Abbey, and in 973, King Edgar was crowned in its Church by Archbishop Dunstan; on which occasion various liberties and privileges were granted to the inmates of that house, and to the inhabitants of the town.

From the general survey of the kingdom, called the *Domesday-Book*, it appears that Bath was held in demesne by William the Conqueror in 1086; that it then contained 178 burgesses, besides six unoccupied houses; and that the annual rent, or fee-farm, paid to the crown, was sixty pounds by tale, and one mark of gold: in addition to which, the mint paid yearly one hundred shillings.

After the Norman Conquest, Bath derived much additional importance from its monastic establishment. The abundant collection of relics possessed by the inmates of that house, and the salubrity of the waters in and near the town, attracted, in those early times, innumerable pilgrims and visitors: for whose accommodation, houses and hostelries were erected, and baths were constructed. Its celebrity was also much increased about the end of the eleventh century, when the Monastery, with the greater part of the town, having been plundered and burnt by the partisans of Robert, Duke of Normandy, were granted by William Rufus, to John de Villula, Bishop of Wells, in augmentation of the diocese of Somersetshire, and for the purpose of transferring the episcopal seat to this place. Under the superintendence of that prelate, and by means of the wealth which he had acquired by practising the medical profession, the newly-established City and Cathedral Church were speedily re-erected, and the former was endowed with important privileges, by the reigning monarch, and by his successor, Henry the First. Immediately after King Stephen's accession to the throne, the whole City, together with St. Peter's Church, are said to have been destroyed by fire. The latter was probably rebuilt by *Robert,* then Bishop of the diocese. About this time, also, the removal of the seat of the prelate from Wells to Bath, caused great dissensions between the Canons of the former city, and the Monks of the latter: "the Canons affirming that the translation of the See by John de Villula could not be held good, because it was made against their consent. The dispute was eventually referred to Bishop Robert, who decreed that the Bishops should neither derive their title from *Wells,* as of old, nor from *Bath,* as in modern times, but that they should in future take their names from both churches, and be called *Bishops* of BATH-and-WELLS: that the Monks of Bath and the Canons of Wells should, on a vacancy of the See, appoint an equal number of delegates, by whose votes the Bishop should be chosen, (the Dean of Wells being the returning officer,) and that he should be enthroned in both churches."*

From the year 1165 to 1174, the City of Bath was retained by Henry the Second, who, in the latter year, granted it, together with the Bishopric, to *Reginald Fitz Joceline:* on whose death in 1191, *Savaric,* a relation of the Emperor of Germany, having been promoted to this See with the annexation of the Abbey of Glastonbury, (as one of the conditions of King Richard's release from captivity,) assumed the title of Bishop of *Bath and Glastonbury,* and granted the Archdeaconry of Bath to the Prior and Convent of the latter Abbey. But in 1193, whether voluntarily or by compulsion is unknown, Savaric resigned the City, then valued at £100 yearly, to the King. Shortly afterwards, that monarch granted to the inhabitants a charter, whereby those who were of the Guild-Merchant were freed from all kinds of tolls and exactions. This charter was confirmed with additional privileges by Henry the Third: in the early part of whose reign the City was leased to the Prior of Bath for the yearly sum of £30; and it appears that in 1235-6 he was compelled to pay £13. 11s. beyond his rent, for the repairs of the King's houses and baths, which had been neglected, and were much dilapidated. About this time Bath again became subordinate to Wells, in "episcopal authority and power."

During the early part of Edward the First's government, the City was assigned in dower to Queen Eleanor: but was subsequently granted, in perpetual alms, by that monarch, to the Bishop of the diocese, in exchange for the patronage of the Abbey of Glastonbury. In 1297-8, the citizens of Bath first returned members to parliament. By Edward the Second, the original charters of the City were confirmed, and additional privileges were granted. The franchises of the inhabitants were also extended by his successor; in the forty-seventh year of whose reign, the tenth paid by them towards carrying on the wars in France was £13. 6s. 8d, whilst the burgesses of the neighbouring

* Britton's "History and Antiquities of Bath Abbey Church," p. 32.

town of Bristol paid £220. Three years afterwards, the men of Bath complained that the people of Bristol injured their trade, and prevented the sale of their merchandise, by holding a fair on the same day as themselves. A remedy was therefore granted them by parliament. From a return of the collectors of the poll-tax in 1377, it appears that the City of Bath then contained only 570 lay inhabitants ; whilst the ecclesiastics within the Archdeaconry were estimated at 201, beneficed and non-beneficed. About this time, mandates were directed to the Mayor and Bailiffs for the repair of the City walls and towers, which had been allowed to fall to decay.

During several succeeding reigns, the name of Bath seldom appears in the pages of history. Insignificant in size, scanty in population, the quiet resort of invalids alone, it held out no temptation to the partisan during the furious struggles for power which marked the fifteenth century, and it is consequently unnoticed in the barren and confused accounts of those tempestuous times. We learn from various sources that its inhabitants paid their quotas of aids, subsidies, and taxes, and obtained, by purchase or grant from a continued succession of monarchs, various liberties and privileges ;—but beyond this, little is known of the state of the city, or of the affairs of its occupants. In the reign of Henry the Fifth began those dissensions between the Citizens and the Monks of Saint Peter's Abbey which only terminated on the dissolution of that house and the dispersion of its inmates. The latter claimed the right of ringing the Abbey bells, both earlier in the morning and later in the evening than those of the Parish Churches ; this, the former considered an infringement of their rights, and persisted in ringing the bells of their respective Churches, both before and after those of the Abbey had been sounded. So furious a contest arose between the contending parties, that although the royal authority interposed between them, they were never thoroughly reconciled.

Leland, who visited Bath in the reign of Henry the Eighth, states, that it then had four gates: and that the walls by which it was surrounded, contained many Roman antiquities, which he supposed to have been collected and inserted therein, by the Norman architects who constructed the fortifications of the City. The towers by which the outworks had in ancient times been guarded, had all been destroyed, excepting one over the Town Gate, and another called " Gascoyn's Tower." There were three baths, known by the respective appellations of the Cross Bath, the Hot Bath, and the King's Bath: and the inhabitants had been, and then were, chiefly supported by the manufacture of cloth, a trade which was much on the decay.

The citizens, who had long exercised and enjoyed many important liberties and franchises, had not the exclusive privileges which they now possess, till 1590, when they were declared to be a body corporate, and at the same time were authorized to purchase lands: their jurisdiction was also extended much beyond the ancient limits. In the ensuing year, the City was honoured with the presence of Queen Elizabeth, during whose visit various improvements were projected, and partially carried into effect, as appears from a letter written in 1596, and printed in Warner's History of Bath, p. 187. It states that " the Citie of Bathe, being both poore enough and proude enough, hath, since her Highnesse being there, wonderfully beautified itselfe in fine houses for victualling and lodging, but decayes as fast as their ancient and honest trades of merchandize and clothing. The fair Church her Highnesse gave order should be re-edified, stands at a stay; and their common sewer, which before stood in an ill place, stands now in no place, for they have not any at all; which for a towne so plentifullye served of water, in a countrey so well provided of stone, in a place resorted unto so greatly, (being at two times of the yeare, as it were, the pilgrimage of health to all saints,) seemeth an unworthie and dishonourable thing. Wherefore, if your Lordship would authorize me, or some wiser than me, to take a strict account of the money, by her Majesty's gracious graunt gathered and to be gathered, which, in the opinion of manie, cannot be lesse than ten thousand pounds, (though, not to wrong them, I thinke they have bestowed upon the point of 10,000 pounds, abating but one cipher,) I would not doubt of a ruinate Church to make a reverent Church, and of an unsavorie town a most sweet town."

In the succeeding reign, the inhabitants of Bath, who were known to be averse to James's government, were stigmatized for being accessory to the gunpowder plot; one of the conspirators having confessed that he had many meetings at Bath, " about this hellish design." They were consequently watched with great jealousy and suspicion by the government. In the early stages of the civil dissensions, which characterized the reign of Charles the First, this City was fortified by the partisans of the royal cause at an expense of £7000. It was afterwards seized by the parliamentary forces, under Sir William Waller, when Prince Maurice, and the Marquis of Hertford, with a considerable body of forces, advanced towards it, and succeeded in drawing Waller's army to Lansdown Hill. Here the latter erected breastworks; but the Royalists, unwilling to engage in the advantageous position he had selected, retired towards Marshfield. Waller, perceiving this, sent his whole body of horse down the hill, to charge them in the rear and flanks, which they did so effectually, that the royal forces were thrown into disorder. Prince Maurice and the Earl of Caernarvon, however, rallied, and succeeded in routing several bodies of the enemy. They next attempted to seize Waller's cannon, which were advantageously planted on the top of a hill, the declivity of which was occupied by strong bodies of the enemy, flanked on either side by a thick wood. The contest was for some time maintained with equal vigour by both armies: but at length, *Sir Belville Grenville*, with a party of horse, a detachment of infantry, and a body of pikemen, bore down all opposition, and gained the brow of the eminence, where that gallant leader was slain. The enemy in the mean time retreated behind a stone wall on the same level, and both parties suspended their operations for a time. During the night, Waller retreated with his army to Bath, leaving possession of the field, and a large portion of his artillery, to the enemy. He was again defeated in a subsequent battle, and the City of Bath was recovered by the royalists; in whose possession it remained till June, 1645, when, through the treachery of the governor, as it is asserted, the republicans again succeeded in taking it. A monument is raised to the memory of Grenville, on Lansdown.

General Fairfax, indignant at the loyalty of the citizens, exacted from them such disproportionate levies, and burdened them with the maintenance of so many troops, that early in the ensuing year they petitioned Mr. John Harrington, who was a staunch republican, to exert his influence in their favor. From a letter written to Captain Harrington, son of the above-mentioned gentleman, in the same year, it appears that the desired redress was obtained. After thanking him for quartering his own troop in the City, it says,—"Many citizens had no monies ready, and were threatened with pillage. Eighteen horses were provided at the market-house, and delivered up as you desired; but the men required were excused on your desiring, nor was any seizure made, or plunder, except in liquors and bedding. Our meal was taken by the Marlborow troop, but they restored it again to many of the poorer sort. Our beds they occupied entirely, but no greater mischief has happened as yet. We have no divine service; the churches are full of the troops, furniture, and bedding. I have sent this by a poor man, who may suffer if he is found out, and I dare not send a man on purpose on horseback, as the horse would be taken."

Although a strong royal party seems to have existed in Bath, it was not until the death of Cromwell, in 1658, that they ventured to declare their principles : but no sooner had the second Charles ascended the throne, than they presented congratulatory addresses, exhibited processions in honour of the event, and in various ways manifested their loyalty and attachment to the new monarch.

In 1646, the City Magistrates, under the authority of Queen Elizabeth's charter, convened a common council, to enact various by-laws for the regulation of tradesmen and others, also for the better management of the baths, cleansing of the streets, and for the general improvement of the City. These ordinances were, in after years, strictly attended to, and the beneficial result has extended to the present time.

In 1663, the King, attended by his brother the Duke of York, the Duchess of Clarence, Prince Rupert, and a numerous assemblage of the nobility, visited the City; when the monarch, in gratitude for the loyalty exhibited by its inhabitants towards his father and himself, confirmed their original charters, and granted them a new one with additional privileges. At the same time, the royal physician, Sir Alexander Frazer, finding that the waters of the place might be used internally with advantage to the patient, recommended their general use; so that, according to **Warner**, "the epoch of drinking the hot waters of Bath, may be fixed to the time of Charles the Second's visit to this City."

During the reign of the ill-omened bigot, James the Second, some of the citizens of Bath, who had favoured the cause of the Duke of Monmouth, were executed, under a warrant from the infamous judge Jeffries. This document contains the following passages :

"These are to will and require yo$^w$ to erect a gallows in the most publike place of yo$^r$ cittie, to hang the said trayto$^{rs}$ on, and that yo$^w$ provide halters to hang them with, a sufficient number of faggots to burne the bowells of fower trayto$^{rs}$, and a furnace or cauldron to boyle their heads and quarters, and salt to boyle therewith, half a bushell to each trayto$^r$, and tarr to tarr y$^m$ with, and a sufficient number of speares and poles, — to fix their heads and quarters."

In 1692, Bath was visited by the princess, afterwards Queen Anne, who was received with every mark of respect by the Mayor and Corporation; but the reigning Queen, with whom Anne was then on bad terms, commanded them in future to refrain from paying more ceremony to her than to any other person. After her accession to the throne, Queen Anne again visited Bath, on which occasion, one hundred young men of the City, uniformly clad and armed, and two hundred young women attired like Amazons, met the Queen and her retinue on the borders of the county, and accompanied them (by a road cut for the occasion from the summit of Lansdown) to the Western Gate of the City, where the royal party were received by the members of the Corporation, and conducted to their lodgings. The concourse of visitors attracted to Bath, in consequence of the Queen's presence, caused a rise of nearly one hundred per cent. in the price of provisions, and one guinea per night was paid for a bed.

Bath had previously been visited only by persons on account of its waters: "the pleasures it afforded were merely rural, the company splenetic, rustic, and vulgar:" but about this time it became frequented by people of distinction. The salubrity of the waters had been praised by Doctor Jordan, and several other eminent physicians, and were consequently used by an increased number of invalids: a summer retreat was wanted, where the more wealthy classes could assemble together, and enjoy the then prevalent amusement of gaming; and Bath seemed fixed upon by general consent for that purpose. The company had hitherto been content with roaming about the romantic walks near the City, and with dancing on the bowling green to the music of a fiddle and hautboy; but about two years after Queen Anne's visit, the amusements were put under the direction of a master of the ceremonies, and conducted with more regularity. Still, however, the diversions were neither elegant nor rational. General society was not established; the nobility refused to keep company with the gentry at any of the public entertainments; smoking was permitted in the public rooms; ladies and gentlemen appeared at the assemblies in aprons and boots; and dancing and gaming were often continued until the morning. In addition to these drawbacks, the lodgings were mean, though expensive; the floors were coloured brown with soot and beer, to hide the dirt; and the furniture was of a common and clumsy kind. The City was also of comparative insignificance; its buildings covered little more than fifty acres of ground; there were no public edifices of importance or beauty; nor were there any wide streets, squares, or crescents: the Pump-house was without a director, and visitors could not walk about after dark without being liable to insult.

Such was the state of things, when Mr. Richard Nash, commonly called Beau Nash, first visited Bath; and under his auspices were commenced those various improvements which have progressively rendered this City one of the most gay, fashionable, and attractive in Europe.

The amusements began to be conducted with regularity,—an officer was appointed to take charge of the Pump-room,—upwards of seventeen hundred pounds were expended in repairing the roads, near the City,—the streets were better paved, cleansed, and lighted,—and invalids were exempted from tolls on entering and going out of Bath. Large houses and broad streets were also built, and adorned with every species of architectural ornament, and the suburbs were laid out in pleasure-grounds and gardens. From that time therefore, Bath became the summer rendezvous of persons of all classes, and was occasionally visited by various members of the Royal family. Until within the last eighty years, the City was principally confined within its ancient walls, and included only the parishes of St. Peter and St. Paul, St. James, and St. Michael; but owing to the celebrity of its waters, and consequent increase of visitors and public amusements, it became necessary to provide suitable accommodations for their reception. New streets were therefore projected, and erected with astonishing rapidity; squares, parades, crescents, and a circus, arose in quick succession; and no measure was neglected which was thought likely to add importance to the City, or to increase its attractions.

The person to whom modern Bath is chiefly indebted for its architectural arrangements, designs, and character, is *Mr. John Wood,* architect. Early in the eighteenth century, he designed and carried into effect the Circus, and many of those buildings which now form the chief ornaments of the City. The first street built under his superintendence was Berton or Barton street: afterwards he constructed a row of houses for James, Duke of Chandos, and about the same time entered into a contract for completing a Canal between Bath and Bristol. During the execution of these works, a person named Strachan was employed to lay out some land on the west side of the City into streets, and Mr. Wood was also engaged to make a plan for covering the Bowling Green, and the Abbey Orchard, with houses. In 1727, the latter architect made designs for rebuilding the whole City conformably to a uniform plan, and not to make small and unconnected additions; but the members of the Corporation slighted his scheme, and he contracted with Mr. Gay for the land on which he subsequently erected *Queen Square.* Barton-street was next extended about one hundred and fifty feet more to the west than originally intended, and a new line of buildings, called John-street, was constructed. He next built the *Lower Rooms* on the east side of the Old Bowling Green, and increased the Terrace-walk in front of it. The success attending this project induced the Corporation to level and plant *Orange Grove,* which had previously been considered a public nuisance. In addition to the buildings above-mentioned, several new streets were formed in the meadows to the west. In the year 1738, a new Act of Parliament was obtained for paving, watching, cleansing, and lighting the streets of the City, and also to regulate the fares of the chairmen. On this occasion there were some peculiar privileges and advantages obtained for the inhabitants in the eastern part of Bath, which was materially improved and augmented in buildings, in consequence. The Abbey Orchard also became the site of many improvements. The North and South Parades, with their interesting avenues, Duke-street and Pierrepont-street, and other buildings, were consequently erected. A line of houses was also commenced fronting the Terrace-walk in King's Mead, Walcot-street; many other rows of houses were extended to the north; and the foundation of a general Hospital was laid near the wall which bounded the City on that side. Shortly afterwards various alterations were made in the Baths; the Old Shambles were converted into a commodious flesh-market; and some additions were made to the Lower Assembly Rooms. The *Circus*, which forms so distinguished a feature of Bath, was also designed by the elder Mr. Wood, who, during his professional career, either erected, or contracted to cover with houses a space of land nearly three times the extent of the original City. The Crescent, Upper Assembly Rooms, and many public edifices, and private houses in various parts of the City, owe their origin to the son of Mr. Wood. Other architects have followed their example; and streets, crescents, and parades have been erected in endless succession: but, to trace the progressive though rapid increase of buildings on the western side of the Avon, would require more space than can here be allotted.

Whilst Bath was thus extended in every direction to the west of the river, Sir William Pulteney, who possessed a large tract of land on the opposite side, did not suffer it to remain unoccupied. He first constructed a lofty Bridge, with houses on it, and then built Laura Place, Great Pulteney-street, and part of Sydney Place, with some of the neighbouring streets. The building of the *Sydney Tavern*, and planting of its gardens, was another novelty, which perhaps contributed more to the entertainment of the Bath visitors than any other recent addition to that City; and although the grounds have been encroached upon by the Kennet-and-Avon Canal, which passes through them, the effect is scarcely perceptible, and certainly not destructive to the beauty and character of the gardens. Sir William Pulteney's daughter, the late Countess of Bath, completed the buildings commenced by her father; and her heir, the Earl of Darlington, has continued to enlarge and carry on the designs of his predecessors.

The improvement of Bath has been manifested not only by the erection of buildings in new situations, but by the altering, widening, and rendering commodious and convenient, the streets of the old part of the City. An Act of Parliament was obtained in 1789, whereby certain commissioners, therein named, were empowered to adopt precautions for preserving the Bath waters, to erect new streets, &c. Cheap-street and Westgate-street have consequently been widened, and other thoroughfares have been improved; but amongst the most prominent and beneficial effects of the above-mentioned Act, may be noticed the erection of *Union-street*, which now forms a convenient communication from the north parts of the City to the Pump-rooms, the building of *Bath-street* and *New Bond-street*, and the improvements in Horse-street on the one side, and in Walcot and Northgate streets on the other, the two chief entrances to the city.  The unsightly old houses, which stood in front of the Guildhall, have been removed; Quiet-street has been widened, and ornamented by a Bazaar and other buildings; a new Hospital has been erected on the ancient site of Belltree Lane; the row of dilapidated houses on the Widcombe-side of the Old Bridge has been demolished; and the alteration, or rebuilding of the Bristol Bridge itself, with many other improvements, are in progress, or in preparation.  A new Bridge has recently been erected over the Avon, at the eastern end of the City, to make a better entrance from the London road.  The Abbey Church, the most interesting building in Bath, was, at no remote period, a public thoroughfare; and its north and south sides were not only obscured, but injuriously built against, by several small houses and shops.  Most of these have been taken down, and the Corporation, as well as Earl Manvers, to whom the property belongs, have very liberally consented to relinquish their rents and profits, for the purposes of public improvement.  The site of the Lower Rooms is occupied by a handsome modern building, appropriated to the " *Bath Literary and Scientific Institution.*"  On the brow of Lansdown Hill, Mr. Beckford has built a lofty and elegant Tower, with some splendid rooms attached; and has also laid out a large tract of the same down in plantations, pleasure-grounds, and gardens.

MUNICIPAL GOVERNMENT.—The Corporation of Bath exercise their authority and jurisdiction under Queen Elizabeth's charter of 1590, to which some additional powers were added in 1794.  Their revenues are derived chiefly from the rent of the pumps, from the profits arising from the private baths in Stall-street, the sums paid by the inhabitants for water, ground rents, and fines for the renewal of leases of City property.  Out of the sums arising from the above-mentioned sources, £1000 is allowed to the chief magistrate during the year of his mayoralty.  The judicial and other business of the City is transacted in the Guildhall, where the Sessions are held four times in each year.  The magistrates have cognizance of all breaches of the peace, and other misdemeanors committed within the liberties.  Personal actions, to the amount of forty shillings, are tried by a Court of Record, which sits every Monday; and a Court of Requests, for the recovery of debts under ten pounds, is held on Wednesdays.  For the better prevention of theft and other crimes, an institution for the apprehension and prosecution of felons, under the name of the " *Bath Society of Guardians,*" was established about the year 1800; and another society, for the same object, termed the "*Bath Forum Association,*" has since been formed.  The *Prison* is a commodious building near Pulteney Bridge; and the *Penitentiary*, established in 1805, is situated in Lady Mead, Walcot-street.

There are in Bath seven Churches of the established religion, and eight Chapels, viz. the Abbey Church of St. Peter, (commonly called the *Abbey*,) Saint Michael's Church; the Parish Church of Walcot; Christ's Church, Montpelier Row; the New Free Church in James-street, dedicated to the Holy Trinity; the Parish Church of Lincombe and Widcombe; and St. Mary's Church, Bathwick.  The Chapels are, St. Michael's Chapel, near the Cross Bath; Queen Square Chapel; the Octagon Chapel, in Milsom-street; St. Margaret's Chapel, Brook-street; All Saints' Chapel, Lansdown Grove; Kensington Chapel, near the London Road, Walcot; Laura Chapel, Henrietta-street; and the Chapel of St. Mary Magdalen, under Beechen Cliff. The Catholics, and following sects of Dissenters, have also places of worship in Bath,—the Baptists, Huntingtonians, Independents, Methodists, Moravians, Quakers, and Unitarians.

The *Public Benevolent Institutions* are, the Hospital; City Infirmary and Dispensary; the Casualty Hospital; the Puerperal, or Child-bed Charity; the Society for the Relief of Poor Married Lying-in Women; the Humane Society; and the Eye Infirmary; the Bimberries, or Hospital of St. Catharine; St. John's Hospital, or the Blue Alms; and Partis College, a large and handsome edifice to the west of the city. There is a Penitentiary, conducted on a plan similar to that of the Magdalen Hospital, London; a public Grammar School; a Charity, or Blue School; Sunday Schools; Catholic Free Schools; an establishment called the Sunday School Union; and an Adult School Society. The public Societies are both numerous and useful.

Amongst the *Places of Amusement* may be enumerated the Assembly Rooms, Concert Rooms, Theatre, and Sydney Gardens; but the chief objects of attraction are the *Baths* and *Pump-rooms*. Though Bath owes its chief celebrity and property to its warm waters, it cannot but excite surprise and regret that the appearance of the Baths, and the accommodations for their visitants, have not been sufficiently studied and respected. It is full time that the Corporation should direct their attention and income to these objects.

Of the eminent literary characters, who were either natives or denizens of Bath, the following are held in high and deserved estimation, not only by their descendants, but by the reading and scientific world in general. Early in the seventeenth century, Jones, Venner, Jorden, Johnson, and Pierce, all resident physicians of Bath, attempted, by their writings, to advance medical science, and give publicity to the waters. Dr. Mayow, who wrote a Chemical Treatise on Nitrous Salts, and Dr. Guidot, a man of extensive knowledge, and a correspondent with the most eminent physicians of his age, were also inhabitants of that city. Early in the next century, we meet with the names of Cheyne, and the two Olivers, who, by communicating to the public the result of their inquiries, eminently adorned the profession of which they were members. These were succeeded by Doctors Falconer and Parry, who to a practical knowledge of medicine added an extensive acquaintance with general literature; and their successor, Sir William Watson, rendered himself eminent, not only by his professional abilities, but by his ardent love of philosophical pursuits. To him that celebrated astronomer, Herschel, who for many years resided in Bath, was indebted for an introduction to his late Majesty, and to the scientific world. Bath was also, at different periods, the place of residence of the celebrated *Botanists*, Dr. Johnson, Sole, and Stackhouse: it may also be regarded as the cradle of English Geology, towards which science, the strata in its immediate vicinity gave the first hints. Mr. Smith is said to have first observed that each layer, or stratum, had its own peculiar fossils, and that the disposition of the strata coincided with the dispositions of those in other parts of the island.

Amongst the *theological* writers who have been natives of, or resided in this City, are the "ever memorable" John Hales, Dr. Samuel Chandler, one of the ablest defenders of revelation, and Bishop Warburton, who there composed "The Divine Legation of Moses demonstrated." We may also mention Melmoth, Bowdler, and Hartley, who, together with Jardine, Maclaine, Cogan, and Simpson, were eminently distinguished for their controversial writings. Amongst the historical authors to whom Bath has given birth, may be enumerated William Prynne, "the devoted investigator of our charter antiquities," Carte, the lecturer of the Abbey, and one of the most authentic English historians, Mrs. Macauley, and Chapman, Wood, Warner, and Lysons, have each exerted their talents in investigating the topographical history and antiquities of that ancient City. To these may be added the names of Pownall, Luders, Leman, and Hunter, who have jointly and severally rendered their names deservedly estimable in the literary annals of their country. Bath has always had its musicians; from Lichfield, the lutanist to Queen Elizabeth, to Rauzini, the eminent composer. Amongst its artists we find Hoare and Gainsborough; and amongst those celebrated in the histrionic art, Siddons, Murray, Knight, Edwin, Russ, Wallace, Elliston, and others. Samuel Daniel wrote the tragedy of Philotas for the Bath stage, as early as the reign of James the First; Sir John Harington, his contemporary, translated the poem of 'Ariosto' into English; the names of Sylvester, Davors, and Allen, may also be quoted: Fielding long resided in the vicinity of that City, and Smollett has successfully represented its local peculiarities in his popular novel of Humphry Clinker. The Sheridans, Linleys, Thicknesse, Graves, Harington, Lee, and Piozzi, are also celebrated in the annals of literature. One name remains, a name that never vibrates on the ear acquainted with Bath, but to produce pleasing associations; that is, *Anstey*, "in whose poem, so truly original, so truly comic, the peculiarities of that City will descend to the latest posterity, and which, as long as the English language endures, will be valued like the plays of Aristophanes."*

* "*The New Bath Guide*," by Mr. Anstey, has been exceedingly popular; nearly twenty editions having passed through the press since its first appearance in 1766. A new and elegant edition of this work, with embellishments, and notes, biographical, topographical, and descriptive, by Mr. Britton, is now in the press. (1829.)

———————————

BATH, FROM BEACHEN CLIFF.

THE GUILDHALL AND CATHEDRAL, FROM THE HIGH STREET.
BATH

# BATH:

## GENERAL VIEW, FROM BEECHEN CLIFF.

Among the numerous pleasing excursions with which the neighbourhood of Bath abounds, none are superior in interest to those of its eastern vicinity; and of these the most attractive terminates near the place where this View is taken. Our journey commences by passing over the Bridge, to Laura Place, Great Pulteney-street, Bathwick, and thence to Bath-Hampton, from which village we are conducted either to the race-ground by ascending the hill on the right, or pass on through a range of beautiful meadows near the river, to the village of Claverton. A considerable degree of interest is given to the handsome Parsonage-house in this village, from the recollection that it was formerly inhabited by the Rev. R. Graves, author of numerous miscellaneous writings, and the friend of Shenstone; and in this rural church-yard is the humble monument of Ralph Allen, Esq. of Prior Park.* If the beautiful scenes which have given so much interest to this short excursion, do not determine us to retrace our steps, we shall proceed over Claverton Downs, and after enjoying many pleasing views of the city, arrive at the noted station of Beechen Cliff, which commands an extensive prospect of Bath, with the Abbey Church nearly in the centre, forming a most interesting object in the picture; and surrounded in every direction by extensive ranges of elegant houses: beyond the Abbey Church appears the Circus, the Crescent, Marlborough Buildings, and St. James's Square; with Camden Place to the right, toward the London road; and other splendid public buildings.

## THE GUILDHALL; AND THE CATHEDRAL, OR ABBEY CHURCH, FROM HIGH-STREET.

No town in England, except the Metropolis, equals Bath in the elegance of its public buildings, which are composed of a beautiful free-stone, from the inexhaustible quarries by which it is surrounded. This stone extends deep into the earth, and is divided into strata of considerable thickness, and these subdivided by fissures into rectangular blocks of great magnitude.

In 1625, a Town-hall was erected in High-street; it was of the Doric and Ionic orders, placed one upon the other, and raised upon six arches on either side, and two on each end: the plan was by the celebrated Inigo Jones. In the front were statues of the Anglo-Saxon kings, Offa and Edgar, reputed benefactors of the city.

* A gentleman eminently distinguished by exemplary piety, benevolence, and every Christian virtue.

In 1776, the first stone of a new Guildhall was laid; but the undertaking was abandoned till 1775, when new designs were procured, and Mr. Thomas Baldwin was employed to complete it: this was effected in 1777, and the old Hall taken down.    In its external appearance, as well as its internal arrangement, the new building possesses great excellence.    It has two fronts, with wings extending fifty feet on each side: the front towards High-street is of the Composite order, and highly ornamental to this part of the city; the other front, facing the Market, is less advantageously situated; but it is equally elegant.    The basement story contains a large and convenient kitchen, above which is the ground-floor, comprising a justiciary-room, with a vestibule; a drawing-room for the Mayor; the Town Clerk's office; a Record-room; a common Clerk's office; a withdrawing room for the Jury; a Deputy Town Clerk's office; and a lobby, near the grand staircase, for the Mayor's officers.    Above these is a magnificent banqueting-room, 80 feet in length, 40 wide, and 31 feet high, of perfect workmanship, and superbly finished. Adjoining to it there is a common-council room.    A very fine antique head of Minerva, originally brass-gilt, and with other interesting relics dug up in Stall-street in 1727, ornaments a chimney-piece in the banqueting-room: there are also in this apartment fine portraits of George III. and his Consort, the Prince and Princess of Orange; the first Earl of Chatham, who was a Representative, and the first Earl Camden, who was a Recorder of Bath.    There is also a fine bust of his late Majesty in his fiftieth year, by Turnerelli; and a portrait of his Royal Highness Frederick Prince of Wales.    An elegant and magnificent silver-gilt cup and salver was presented by this Prince to the Corporation, as a testimony of the grateful sense his Royal Highness retained of the attention paid to him, when at Bath in 1737.    This cup passes round at all public entertainments with great ceremony.—The sessions are held quarterly, in the Guildhall, and take cognizance of misdemeanors; the court of record also sits every Monday, and determines in all personal actions of forty shillings amount and upwards.    The banqueting-room is used every fortnight, during the season, for the city balls, and the adjoining room for the card assemblies; a master of the ceremonies presiding.

Immediately contiguous to the Guildhall is the public Market-house, built in the theatric form, and very convenient.    The market-days are Wednesdays and Saturdays; on which days the greatest abundance of all the necessaries of life are found, as well as luxuries and delicacies of every description; and on all days of the week (except Sunday) this market is well supplied.    The butter of Bath is of peculiar excellence; the vegetables in the greatest variety and perfection; and the shambles and poultry-stalls, of cleanly appearance and convenient arrangement.

BATH ABBEY CHURCH.

WESTON BRIDGE, NEAR BATH.

## THE ABBEY CHURCH.

This is now the only church within the parish of St. Peter and St. Paul; but the original parochial church was that of St. Mary Stall, which formerly stood where a range of houses are now built, by the Pump-room Piazza. This church, with the parish of Widcombe, were given to the Prior and Monks of Bath, in the year 1236, by William Button, Bishop of Wells. The first Vicar of Stall was John de Dudmarton, appointed by the Monastery of Bath in 1322, with the appropriation of the parishes of Widcombe, Lyncombe, and Berewycke, for his support. There remains no record of any other presentation till the 30th of Henry VIII. which seems to have been the last; for soon afterwards, the Prior William Holloway, and the Monks of Bath, granted the advowson of the church of St. Mary Stall, to Sir Walter Denys. It remained vested in the crown, after the Dissolution, till 1573, when the parishes of St. Michael, St. James, and those of Walcot, Widcombe, and Lyncombe, were added to that of St. Mary, and consolidated into a Rectory by Archbishop Grindal, (the See of Wells and Bath being at that time vacant,) under letters patent of Queen Elizabeth. The patronage was vested in the Corporation of Bath, who soon afterwards pulled down the fine old church of St. Mary Stall.

This noble building of the Abbey Church, justly esteemed the glory and ornament of Bath, was begun in 1495, and finished in 1606: it occupies the ancient foundation of the original conventual church erected by King Osric, in 676; and was begun in the time of Henry VII. by Oliver King, bishop of the Diocese: but according to Fuller, this good bishop only lived to see the west end nearly finished, and curiously carved with angels climbing up a ladder to heaven, agreeable to the visionary appearance by which he had been led to the undertaking. After his death the building was neglected, and we are informed that some person wrote with charcoal, on its decaying walls, the following triplet :—

> O Church! I wail thy woeful plight,
> Whom *King*, nor *Cardinal*, nor *Clark*, nor *Knight*,
> Have yet restor'd to ancient right.

Alluding to Bishop King and his four successors, during thirty-five years, viz. Cardinals Adrian and Wolsey, and Bishops Clark and Knight. The Commissioners of Henry VIII. sold the glass and iron, with the lead, weighing 480 tons, leaving nothing but the bare walls. Mr. Peter Chapman was the first person who began to repair it, about the year 1572, securing the roof from the effects of the weather; yet little was done toward its re-edification, till Burleigh, Lord Treasurer to Elizabeth, patronized the undertaking, and completed the choir, for public worship: on which occasion the following poetico-prophetic lines were chalked up :—

> Be blithe, fair Kirk, when HEMPE is past,
> Thine OLIVE, that ill winds did blast,
> Shall flourish green for age to last.

The monogram, HEMPE, is formed of the initials of Henry VIII., Edward VI., Mary and Philip, and Elizabeth. The prediction was verified, when Bishop Montague, joined by Sir Henry Montague, Lord Chief Justice, and several other noblemen and gentlemen, completed this admirable building; which may be considered the last specimen of the ecclesiastic Gothic architecture in England, as it was erected when the style prevailed and flourished in great beauty and purity.

The grand entrance, by a descent of four steps, through the noble arch of the west end, is in the highest degree picturesque, as the expanding view takes in the whole of the interior. Uniformity, proportion, and harmony, characterize every part of this beautiful fabric; its clustered columns and piers, its wide expansive windows elegantly arched, produce a pleasing airy lighness, seldom seen in similar buildings. The western door was given by Sir Henry Montague, in 1617; it is charged with the arms of the See, impaling those of Montague, with the device of the Order of the Garter round the shield: two upper shields bear the arms of Montague only, under which is a label, inscribed " *Ecce quam bonum, et quam jucundum,*" &c. Above is a profile helmet, with a crest of a Griffin's head; behind is a flowing mantle, and at the bottom of the door are two ornamental bosses: these devices are strikingly characteristic of the decorative style of architecture, which began to decline soon after this building was finished.

Numerous mouldings compose the architrave of the entrance, from which a sub-architrave diverges, forming a square head above the arch. Wounded hearts, feet, and hands, with crowns of thorns, representing the Saviour's sufferings, ornament the labels which cover the spandrels of the arch. The statues of St. Peter and St. Paul stand on each side, on brackets, in niches, richly canopied. Under the feet of St. Peter appears the conjoined red and white roses, and a crown: a crown is also under St. Paul, with a portcullis. The characteristic attributes of the patron saints are nearly destroyed. Over the head of the arch a slender cornice supports an open battlement, elegantly formed, divided in the centre, in which there is a niche, once enclosing the statue of Henry VII.; but the arms and supporters are all that now remain. The turrets are quadrangular in the first divisions, on each side of which are narrow openings, to give light to the staircase within: on the front of the upper part ladders appear, with angels ascending, representative of the bishop's vision. On each side of the ladder figures of men, habited as shepherds, may yet be discerned, with labels over their heads, the inscriptions on which are quite obliterated. The turrets are octangular in their second divisions, and the ladders are continued, with the busts of two saints over their tops, each holding an open book. Statues of the twelve Apostles form three tiers on each of the front cants; and the third divisions with their battlements, are in compartments, finishing with open spires.

Richness of workmanship distinguishes the great west window, which has two sub-arches, with a large division between them. The arches, sub-arches, spandrels, and various parts of the window, are equally divided into three parts, in reference, probably, to the mystery of the holy Trinity, represented in material imagery, in the centre of the battlement, with two shields, bearing arms; and tne supporters of Henry VII. holding the united red and white roses, &c. Choirs of angels are seen in the spandrels, singing praises, in attitudes of adoration; an angel is also seen issuing from a cloud, with a shield, the bearings defaced. The architrave forms the entire line of the window, and the sub-architrave forms the boundary of the head, beginning at the springing of the arch. Two shields of arms are seen among the angels, charged with two bendlets dexter, embattled and counter-embattled, and surmounted by a cardinal's hat. This is understood to be Cardinal Adriano Castella; his arms are on each side of the centre of the upper division of the choir. The lines of the battlements, and the cornice above the spandrels, are pedimental, and the same beautiful open tracery ornaments the battlements, as are seen below. The buttresses on each side of the windows are ornamented with rolls, over which are arched heads, their supporters bearing the arms of Henry VII. with the regal crown, from the rays of which spring olive-trees, surmounted by bishops' mitres. Similar devices, or a repetition of these, occur, till we come to the windows entering the side aisles, which, in conformity to the central entrance, bear on the spandrels crowns of thorns, &c. On their mullions are statues, standing on pedestals, under canopies: one of these is our Saviour holding a scroll with seals in one hand, and with the other pointing to the wound in his side; the other is King Edgar, holding up a bag of money.

These windows are ornamented in the same manner as the larger ones, somewhat plainer, but very beautiful. That part of the roof which extends over the nave is evidently of later construction than that of the choir, and rises higher; yet, by its projecting groins, forms a deeper arch, and descends lower in its open workmanship, displaying the most beautiful ramifications. The ribs which compose the tracery of the roof constitute the only solid part, the spaces, formerly cut through and left open, having been filled up since with common laths and plaster. Its windows, fifty-two in number, large and elegant, with its open roof, gave to this airy fabric a lightness consistent with, and accounting for, the appellation given to it of " The Lantern of England." Twelve clustered pillars separate the side aisles from the nave, supporting elliptical arches, very flat; the span thirty feet ten inches, and the elevation only three feet. Stone pillars support a wooden screen, which separates the nave from the choir; and above this is an exceedingly fine-toned organ. This church measures from east to west 210 feet; from north to south, 126; across the body and aisles, 72 feet; and from the point where the transept, nave, and choir unite, springs a noble tower, 162 feet high, of a very unusual oblong form; but displaying great architectural skill; surmounted by perforated battlements, forming an appropriate termination of this lofty edifice.

The representation of the Wise Men's Offering, over the altar, in the choir, was given by General Wade, and is well executed. Prior Bird's monument is highly ornamental. This elegant piece of architecture, usually denominated a *Monumental Chapel*, consists of two arched divisions, impost, entablature, and octangular buttresses; the whole richly embellished. At the south west front of this chapel are two elegant ranges of niches, unoccupied, rising from the impost, and terminated by pennailes and spires. The effigy of the munificent Bishop Montague is laid on the top of an altar tomb, in his pontifical habiliments, in the north centre of the nave. The letter W, with the figure of a Bird, which appears on the walls in various places, is a rebus of the name of William Bird, Prior of Bath, who repaired the parts so distinguished. He was Prior in 1499, and died blind and poor, in 1525.

## ENTRANCE TO BATH, FROM THE SOUTH, BY THE OLD BRIDGE.

The first Bridge of Bath was built in the time of Edward the Third; and, previous to its erection, the communication with the opposite side was by a ford, a little higher up the stream. Leland observes of his passing this way into the city—" Or ever I came to Bath Bridge that is over Avon, I came down by a rokky hille, fulle of springes of water; and on this rokky hille is sett a longe streate as a suburbe to the cyte of Bath: and in this streate there is a Chapelle of St. Mary Magdalene. There is a great Gate, with a stone arch, at the entrance of the Bridge." This bridge was taken down in 1754, and very handsomely rebuilt at the expense of the Corporation; it is supported by five arches, and has stone balustrades. The road leading westward follows the course of the river to Bristol; and is the great thoroughfare to that city, and to Wales, not less than forty stage-coaches passing daily: the road in front conducts to Wells, Exeter, and the West of England; and the road passing eastward conducts to Salisbury and Portsmouth.

## THE HOT BATH, AND NEW INFIRMARY.

This Bath takes its denomination from the superior heat of its spring, approaching to 117° of Fahrenheit. It is about forty yards, in a south-westerly direction, from the King's Bath; was built under the superintendence of Mr. John Wood, and is about fifty-six feet square: it has an open bath, a private bath, dry pump-rooms, and vapour-baths, constantly kept warm by flues communicating with the fires of an adjoining dressing-room. This Bath fills in eight hours: the pump-room is a little to the westward, and the entrance being without steps, particularly convenient for those who require to be carried into it. The following poetic effusion is placed over the pump :—

HYGEIA broods with watchful wing,
O'er ancient Badon's mystic spring;
And speeds from its sulphureous source,
The steamy torrent's secret course;
And fans th' eternal sparks of hidden fire,
  In deep unfathom'd beds below,
  By Bladud's magic taught to glow;
Bladud! high theme of Fancy's Gothic lyre.

ENTRANCE TO BATH, FROM SOUTH SIDE OF THE BRIDGE.

THE HOT BATHS, AND NEW INFIRMARY,
BATH.

LITERARY INSTITUTION & CATHEDRAL, FROM NORTH PARADE,
BATH.

THE KING'S BATH PUMP ROOM, AND COLONNADE,
BATH.

# THE LITERARY INSTITUTION.

This useful institution is in the south-eastern part of the City, and occupies a handsome building opposite the Pump-Room of the Duke of Kingston's Baths. The association was formed in 1816: on its first meeting it had nearly one hundred members, and has ever since been well supported. It is similar in its purposes to the scientific institutions of London, Liverpool, Manchester, and Newcastle; and its Lecture Room is supplied with an extensive collection of furnaces, retorts, and every necessary apparatus for experiments and exhibitions to illustrate the various branches of experimental Philosophy, Chemistry, Geology, Mineralogy, and the several arts with which they are connected.

Not only as affording the most rational amusements, but as laying a substantial foundation of useful knowledge in the minds of its younger members, this Institution recommends itself to the opulent manufacturer, the agriculturist, the ingenious mechanic, and to the votaries of science of every class of society.

The following are the RULES of this SOCIETY:

1. That the meetings of the Society be on every Monday evening throughout the year, excepting the months of June, July, August, and September, at half-past seven, and to close at half-past nine.

2. The first part of the evening, not exceeding one hour, to be appropriated to the communication, from any of the members, of different interesting subjects connected with the objects of the Society, and of proposals relative to experiments desired to be tried. The remaining part of the evening to be devoted to the reading and discussion of any paper presented to the Society, or of any communication relative to literature, experimental philosophy, chemistry, geology, mineralogy, mechanics, &c. from any of its members.

3. That each member shall be entitled to introduce each evening, a lady, or a young gentleman, under sixteen years of age; or may be permitted to introduce a friend, if not under the above condition, so that the said friend shall not be introduced more than twice in the same session. No person, not a member, can be admitted without a card signed by the member by whom he is introduced.

4. That all the members of this Society are free to all the lectures delivered by Dr. Wilkinson, in the Kingston Lecture Room.

5. After the first meeting of the Society, each person, subsequently admitted a member, must be recommended by two subscribers to the institution.

6. That there be three presidents, a secretary, and experimentalist.

7. Each member to pay, on his admission, two guineas and five shillings, and the same sum annually.

8. Visitors to Bath may be admitted as members, for three months, upon being properly introduced, and paying one guinea and five shillings.

Ladies and gentlemen disposed to become members, are desired to enter their names in the Society's subscription book, at the Kingston Pump Room.

The session is from the first Monday in October, to the last Monday in May. The subscription of each member to be dated from the period of the name being entered on the books.

## THE KING'S BATH, PUMP ROOM, AND COLONNADE.

In passing from the Abbey along Stall-street, we approach the great Pump Room, with its open Colonnade. Dr. Oliver, in his Treatise on the Bath Waters, in 1704, suggested the necessity of a building for the reception of those who came to drink the waters; and this induced the Corporation to commence the erection of the first Pump Room, which was finished in 1706, and opened under the direction of Mr. Nash, who was at that time appointed master of the ceremonies. In 1751, this building was much enlarged; and it was again rendered more commodious, and embellished with a handsome Portico, in 1786. The western front received considerable improvement, with the addition of an ornamental frontispiece, in 1791; and in 1796 the whole was taken down, and the present Pump Room, erected under the direction of Mr. Baldwin, to whose taste it does great credit. It was also ornamented and improved in 1813. This building is in length 85 feet, in width 46, and in height 34 feet. The internal decorations are in unison with the beauty of its exterior; with conformity of design in its three-quarter columns, its architrave, and crownings. A fine statue of Mr. Nash, by Hoare, and an elegant time-piece, occupy two niches on the eastern end of the room; and on the opposite end is the Music Gallery.

The Pump occupies the central part of the southern side, between two fire-places; the water issuing out of an elegant vase of marble. The public notice of the Governors of the General Hospital, with the highly beautiful Address by the poet Anstey, are inscribed on the Pump, in letters of gold:—

### THE HOSPITAL
OF THIS CITY,

Open to the Sick Poor of every Part of the World,
To whose cases these Waters are applicable,
*(The Poor of Bath only excepted,)*
Was first established, and is still supported, by the charitable
Contributions of the Liberal and Humane.

———

Oh! pause awhile, whoe'er thou art,
That drink'st this healing stream;
If e'er compassion o'er thy heart
Diffus'd its heavenly beam;
Think on the wretch whose distant lot
This friendly aid denies;
Think how in some poor lonely cot
He unregarded lies!
Hither the helpless stranger bring,
Relieve his heartfelt woe,
And let thy bounty, like this spring,
In genial currents flow:
So may thy years from grief and pain,
And pining want, be free;
And thou from Heaven that mercy gain,
The poor receive from thee.

Enclosed in a frame, and glazed, are the following Spenserian Stanzas by Dr. Harrington :—

Alwhyle ye drynke, 'midst age and ache ybent,
Ah creepe not comfortless beside our streame,
(Sweet nurse of hope;) affliction's downwarde sente,
Wythe styll smalle voyce, to rouze from thryftlesse dreame;
Each wyng to prune, that shyftythe everie spraie
In wytlesse flyghte, and chyrpythe lyfe awaie.
Alwhyle ye lave—such solace may be founde;
When kynde the hand, why'neath its healynge faynte?
Payne shall recure the hearte's corruptede wounde;
Farre gonne is that which feeleth not its playnte.
By kyndrede angel smote, Bethesda gave
New vyrtues forthe, and felt her troubledde wave.
Thus drynke, thus lave—nor ever more lamente,
Our sprynges but flowe pale anguishe to befriende;
How fayre the meede that followeth contente!
How bleste to lyve, and find such anguishe mende.
How bleste to dye—when sufferynge faith makes sure,
At life's high founte, an everlastynge cure!

This elegant and spacious room is open from an early hour in the morning, till four in the afternoon; and an excellent musical band plays from one till half-past three, during the season.

The King's Bath is a bason of large dimensions, being nearly 66 feet by 41 feet, and, when filled, contains 346 tons, 2 hogsheads, and 36 gallons.  An octagonal enclosure in the centre is surrounded by a brass railing, within which the spring rises with great force ; and from this reservoir the water is distributed in a very pure state to the pumps, for drinking ; at the same time that it fills its own cistern, it also fills that of the Queen's Bath, which joins to it on its southern side.  This Bath was originally built by Mr. Bellot, and retained the name of the New Bath, being appropriated to the use of the poor ; till the year 1615, when the Queen of James the First, being alarmed by a phosphoric light rising from the water, which was considered at that time a supernatural appearance, in the King's Bath, could not be persuaded to bathe in it again, but made use of the New Bath, which on that account was much enlarged and embellished, and received its present name.  Convenient rooms are attached to these Baths, with pumps and pipes to direct the hot water to any particular part of the body.  The basons fill in about eleven hours, and the heat of the water is 116 degrees of Fahrenheit.  The water is retained for the use of the public, from an early hour in the morning till noon : there is a handsome colonnade on one side, to shelter the bathers.

In a recess in the " King's Bath," there is a statue, with the following inscription :—

" BLADUD,
Son of Lud Hudibras,
Eighth King of the Britons from Brute,
A great Philosopher and Mathematician,
Bred at Athens,
And recorded the first Discoverer and Founder of these Baths,
Eight Hundred and Sixty-Three Years before Christ ;
That is,
Two Thousand Five Hundred and Sixty-Two Years
to the present Year,
One Thousand Six Hundred and Ninety-Nine.

MAUDLIN CHAPEL, BATH.

THE CROSS BATH, FROM BATH STREET.

## THE CROSS BATH.

Several new streets were built in Bath in 1789, of which that called Bath-street is not the least elegant : on each side of it there is a colonnade, with rows of Ionic pillars ; and on its opposite extremities are the King's Bath and the Cross Bath : this latter is an elegant building of a triangular form, and has a small neat Pump Room attached to it. It was built from a design by Mr. Baldwin.

The ancient Cross from which this spring derives its name, serves to ascertain the fact, " that the Bath waters were known and used by our Saxon ancestors." It was erected here, as an evidence of the waters being reclaimed from Heathen superstition, to the service of Christ, in conformity to the instructions given by Gregory the Great, to St. Augustine and his associates; which directed, that all the well-built temples, and places dedicated to idols in Britain, should be converted from the worship of devils to the service of the true God, by a solemn consecration, sealed with an image of the Cross of Christ, as the Theodosian law directed. This Cross remained in the Bath till the beginning of November, 1745. The ancient erection, which has given the name of Gregory's Cross to the place so called, near Bath, is believed to have had a similar origin.

In 1755, the foundations of Roman Baths were discovered not far distant from the present Cross and King's Baths. The walls were of wrought stone, lined with strong cement of terras ; one of them was of a semicircular form, 15 feet in diameter, surrounded by a stone seat, and descended by seven steps; the floor was of smooth flag-stones, and a channel to convey away the water passed off in a right line toward the present King's Bath. Not far distant was another very large oblong bath, on three sides of which was a colonnade, probably to support a roof: on one side were two sudatories, of a square form, the floors of brick, covered with strong terras, the fabric supported by pillars of bricks two inches thick and nine inches square. These pillars, $4\frac{1}{2}$ feet high, and 14 inches asunder, formed a *hypocaust* to retain the heated vapour for the rooms above, to which it was communicated by tubulated bricks inserted in the walls ; the fireplace was a conically arched building near the outer wall. There were numerous other apartments ; some of which were peculiar to Roman baths, as, the *Frigidarium*, or undressing-room ; the *Tepidarium*, moderately heated ; and the *Eleathesion*, in which were deposited the ointments and perfumes used by the bathers. These rooms communicated with each other, and were some of them paved with flag-stones, others beautifully tesselated with dies of various colours. Well-formed channels conveyed the superfluous water into the Avon.

These interesting antiquities sufficiently confirm the historical accounts of the occupation of Bath by the Romans in the time of Claudius, about the year 43; and the traces of the Catholic Missionaries in the Saxon æra will scarcely be disputed; but the supposed discovery of these mineral springs by the ancient Britons, and the legend of King Bladud, will remain a subject of interminable dispute.

## MAUDLIN, OR MARY MAGDALEN'S CHAPEL.

A few years ago this Chapel was in ruins, and only interesting to the passing traveller, as a venerable remnant of antiquity; but it has been lately put in complete repair, or rather rebuilt, with the preservation of its ancient Gothic style of architecture—its narrow lancet windows and embattled tower. The original building was of high antiquity; and adjoining to it is a small hospital for lunatics and lepers, said to have been built by Prior Cantilow; but Bishop Tanner believes it to have been much older than his time, and only repaired by him, for on the tenth of June, 1332, the Bishop of Bath and Wells granted an indulgence of twenty days to the benefactors of the Hospital of St. Cross and St. Mary Magdalen, of Bath; and in the will of Hugh Wells, bishop of Lincoln, in the year 1212, besides a legacy to St. John's Hospital, there is a bequest for the use of lepers in the suburbs of Bath. This Chapel was repaired in the year 1760, and the Hospital rebuilt in 1761. The following Inscription, in the porch, preserves the record of Prior Cantilow's repairing this edifice, without mentioning the time; it may, indeed, be a mere revival of the traditionary account.

**INSCRIPTION.**

Thys Chapell floryshyd. wt. formosyte. spectabyll.
In the honowre. of M. Magdalen. Prior Cantylo. hath edyfyde.
Desyringe. yow. to. pray. for. him. wt. yowre.
pryers. delectabyll.
That. sche. will. inhabit. him. in hevyn.
ther. evyr. to abyde.

## THE ROYAL CRESCENT.

The front of this noble pile of building, from its elevated situation, is calculated to attract the attention of strangers. It consists of thirty elegant mansions of freestone, uniformly built. Columns of the Ionic order, rising from a rustic basement, support the superior cornice, and the stately fronts of the houses at each end, add greatly to the

THE ROYAL CRESCENT, BATH.

CAMDEN PLACE, BATH.

general effect: if there be, in the whole, an appearance rather of deficiency than excess of ornament, this is strictly conformable to its general character of grandeur and magnificence. The houses are convenient and tastefully finished, and the form of the apartments not perceptibly injured by the enlarged dimensions of its exterior, compared with the interior circumference; the whole forming only a small part of a very large ellipsis.

The whole extent of the city of Bath is seen from the Crescent, and no other station affords a prospect so extensive and various; Brook-street conducts us westward to the Circus; in front are the Crescent fields, with the vale beyond; the river in its course toward Bristol; the opposite hills in various directions; and numerous surrounding villages. Of the hills seen from the Crescent, Barrow-hill is of the most singular and picturesque appearance. This eminence, as its name imports, is believed to have been, in part, of artificial formation; it is placed on the brow of a high ridge, west of the village of Inglescomb.

A late writer on the scenery of Bath has remarked, that " an evening scene is productive of the most brilliant effects, and the *Crescents* are then seen to the utmost advantage; their situation, their concave form, which catches a variety of light, and their tone of colour, are then peculiarly adapted to the pencil. In the month of January, when the air is frosty, and the sun dropping from the horizon, there is an effect of light and shadow on these buildings, and on the *Circus*, which is not to be described by the pen. The varied forms of the buildings of Bath, and the different elevations on which they stand, add greatly to their picturesque appearance in prospect; which, from a small distance, is equally singular and beautiful."

## CAMDEN PLACE.

At the top of Lansdown-street, on the elevated acclivity of Beacon-hill, is placed this most superb elliptical range of buildings, overlooking all the eastern part of the city, on the one hand; on the other, commanding an extended prospect of the beautiful valley, with the winding stream of Avon, its green meadows, and the handsome villages scattered along its borders. The London Road approaching Bath, passes through a pleasant avenue formed by mountainous elevations on either side, and immediately below is the village of Walcot, consisting formerly of a few scattered rural habitations, but now making part of Bath; its parochial limit, on its highest elevation, containing the greater part of the new buildings of the city in its upper division; and in the lower containing the extensive erections of Grosvenor Buildings, Walcot Parade, St. Mark's Buildings, Walcot Terrace, Kensington Place, Upper and Lower East Hays, Piccadilly, with Walcot Church and Chapel, and numerous elegant buildings.

At a distance, to the south-east, the prospect is diversified by the appearance of Prior Park, with numerous interesting objects; and nearer, in the same direction, are Sydney Gardens, and the splendid architectural embellishments of Bathwick.

## WESTON BRIDGE.

This plain substantial building is formed to harmonize admirably with the surrounding sylvan scenery, which is exceedingly beautiful. The village from which it is named, is at a short distance, and consists of one irregular street, extending about half a mile along a woody vale; a high down rises on the west; Lansdown Hill is on the south-east; and its southern extremity is open to the country. A stream, called Lock's Brook, issuing from the hill, and passing along the whole length of the street, empties itself into the Avon.

This Brook, in its course, separates the parishes of Twiverton and Weston; each of these villages being a mile and a half from the Hot Wells of Bath. In this vicinity there are extensive quarries, in which are found abundance of petrefactions, and curious mineral formations, interesting to naturalists; and, in the western part of the parish, there is a petrifying spring, which quickly forms incrustations on whatever is exposed to its influence. At the western extremity of the village there is a natural cascade of considerable beauty, formed by the descent of a powerful stream from the high grounds. This village, which is chiefly inhabited by laundresses, has a neat and comfortable appearance, the houses being universally built of freestone.

The Church is an appropriate and plain building; but it is surrounded by splendid monuments of genteel and dignified persons, who, dying at Bath, have preferred this rural cemetery to the crowded burying grounds of the City.

Near this village, there is a small settlement of the religious society of *Moravians,* with a chapel, and handsome burying ground.

Weston was the birth-place of the famous, pious, and learned Elphage, Archbishop of Canterbury; who, receiving his education, and rising to eminence in the Benedictine monastery of Deerhurst in Gloucestershire, and residing some time at Bath, was called to the Bishopric of Winchester in 994; from which he was raised to the See of Canterbury in 1006; but the Danes, in 1011, burnt the city and church of Canterbury, and after imprisoning the pious Archbishop for several months, cruelly stoned him to death at Greenwich.

LANSDOWN TOWER, LANSDOWN HILL, NEAR BATH.

BRACKEN CLIFF, FROM THE BANKS OF THE AVON.

## LANSDOWN TOWER.

Lansdown Hill is ornamented by some of the most splendid buildings of Bath; and commands pleasing and extensive prospects into the counties of Somerset, Gloucester, Worcester, Wiltshire, and the mountains of Wales; and on account of the salubrity of its air, convenient walks, and roads for horses and carriages, have been made for the accommodation of invalids.

In 1720, Lord Lansdown, the poet, erected the Tower or Monument, which perpetuates the memory of his grandfather, Sir Bevil Granville, who fell in the severe conflict which took place here between the royal and parliamentary forces, the former commanded by Prince Maurice, the latter by General Waller. The engagement was on the 5th of July, 1643, on the top of the hill, and Sir Bevil was slain on the northern side, where the Monument is erected; the exact spot was ascertained by an old woman, who being a girl at the time, passed over the hill, and across the field of battle.

On the death of the brave Sir Bevil, his son was created Viscount Lansdown, and Earl of Bath; and died in the year 1710. Whilst Charles, his son, was attending his father's funeral, one of his pistols went off, and shot him dead. He was buried at the same time, and succeeded by his son, William Henry; who, dying a minor, the barony passed to the heir of Sir Bevil's second son, Bernard, whose son, George, the poet, was knighted by Queen Anne. On the death of George, without heir, in 1734, the title became extinct. William, Earl of Bath, died in 1623, and the title was given to his eldest son, Edward, from whom it passed, in 1636, to Henry, the heir of the second Earl; and on his death, in 1654, it was conferred on Sir John Granville: it was revived, in 1742, in William Pulteney, Esq. who died in 1764, and his son, John, dying a year before him, the title again became extinct; and, in 1789, the title of Marquis of Bath was given to Thomas Thynne, Viscount Weymouth.

The pillar is of free-stone, and quadrangular, rising from a base of twenty-one feet square. On the south tablet is the following, from Lord Clarendon's history, " In this battle, on the king's part, there were more officers and gentlemen of quality slain, than common men; and more hurt than slain: but that which would have clouded any victory, and made the loss of others less spoken of, was the death of Sir Bevil Granville. He was, indeed, an excellent person, whose activity, interest, and reputation, was the foundation of what had been done in Cornwall; and his temper and affection so public, that no accident which happened could make an impression on him; and his example kept others from taking any thing ill. In a word, a brighter courage and a gentler disposition were never married together, to make the most cheerful and innocent conversation." The western side has a tablet filled with warlike trophies, alluding to the actions of Charles, Earl of Lansdown, in Hungary; these consist of the arms of England, resting upon the joint arms of George, Duke of Albemarle, and John, Earl of Bath, with military ornaments, in allusion to the restoration of Charles the Second; and the following lines commemorate the bravery of Sir Bevil's grandfather, Sir Richard Granville, in the remarkable instance of his fighting the whole Spanish Armada with a single ship, in the Azores, in 1591.

> " Thus slain, thy valiant Ancestor did lye,
> When his one bark a Navy did supply.
> When now emcompass'd round the Victor stood,
> And bath'd his pinnace in his conquering blood,
> Till, all his purple current dry'd and spent,
> He fell, and made the waves his monument.
> Where shall the next fam'd Granville's trophies stand?
> Thy Grandsire's fill the seas, and thine the land."

Under these lines is the following inscription.

> To the immortal Memory of his renowned Grandfather,
> and valiant Cornish Friends,
> Who conquered, dying in the Royal cause, July 5th, 1643,
> This Column was dedicated by the Right Honourable George Granville, Lord Lansdown,
> in the year 1720.
>
> " DULCE EST PRO PATRIA MORI."

## BEACHEN CLIFF.

The area enclosing the Hot Springs of Bath is surrounded by stupendous hills, of a much quicker ascent to the south and to the east, than to the west and the north ; and the surface of the river Avon is, at this place, at least forty feet above that of the Severn sea, toward which, as it flows, numerous streams are carried off to mills of various kinds. Beachen Cliff rises upwards of 360 feet above this river, on the southern side of Bath. This hill appears from the city like a vast heap of earth, whose northern side has been undermined, and made to slip down, leaving a semicircular cliff above it; which is covered with wood.  Its original name was Blake Leigh, and this name is yet retained by the upper part of it.  The ancient names of places were always significant; which is evinced by this instance, the name denoting fertile or cultivated land, in a bleak and exposed situation.

THE OLD BRIDGE, BATH.

PULTENEY BRIDGE, BATH.

The difficulty of ascending the hills of Bath, is by no means so considerable as their height might lead us to suppose; and the beautiful prospects and the salubrious air enjoyed upon them, can no where in any country be exceeded. The walks and rides in different directions amount to between thirty and forty, and various stations affording extensive views, infinitely varied, present themselves. About a mile on the road to Wells, there is a conspicuous building, called Cottage Crescent; from this elevation we have a most luxurious prospect of hills and dales, and the river Avon in its course toward Bristol, with woods and fruitful fields; and to the left, Hampton and Claverton Downs, Prior Park, and many pleasant villages: but if we wish to enjoy a nearer view of Bath, which shall present to the eye more distinctly its various elegant buildings, we must ascend to the summit of Beachen Cliff; looking down from which, this city has been compared to ancient Carthage, as it appeared from the eminence over which it was approached; and the following passage from *Virgil* has been referred to:

> Now o'er the lofty hill they bend their way,
> Whence all the rising town in prospect lay,
> And Towers and Temples; for the mountain's brow
> Hung bending o'er, and shaded all below.
> Where late the cottage stood, with glad surprise
> The Prince beholds the stately palace rise;
> On the paved streets, and gates, looks wondering down,
> And all the crowd and tumult of the town.

## THE OLD BRIDGE.

The institution of monachism originating in a principle of selfishness, appears little calculated to benefit society; yet in after times, under the government of a superintending Providence, the various modifications of this principle were made to contribute to the general welfare, in the then existing state of society; which could scarcely have been effected by any other conceivable means; and some gratitude is due from posterity, to the monks of Bath, not only for their encouragement of industry, but also for the erection of the first bridge over the Avon at this place, to give facility to trade and commerce, and for the general advantage and convenience of the citizens.

William de Marchia, the twelfth Bishop of Bath, holding the high office of Lord Treasurer, obtained a grant from the King, in favour of his Abbey, of two fairs, one in the meadow called the Ham, the other in the parish of Lyncomb, at the top of Holloway, where it has ever since continued to be held.

Over the door of the ancient Abbey-house, there was a figure of a shuttle cut in stone, as an honourable memorial of the first introduction of the manufacture of cloth into Bath, by the Abbot, in the time of Edward the Third, who gave the city its first charter in 1316; when South Gate was rebuilt, with a statue of King Edward over it, supported on one side by the Bishop, and on the other by the Prior of Bath; and to obviate the inconvenience of fording the river, a Bridge was built of stone, to connect the city with the parish of Lyncomb.

On this occasion, the Prior obtained permission to build a Chapel on the bridge, dedicated to St. Lawrence, to catch the attention and the alms of the passengers, either for the repairs of the bridge, or to support the poor, or to enrich the coffers of the Abbey: probably, in part for all these purposes. The original Bridge of St. Lawrence remained entire in Leland's time; but has since been pulled down, and the present bridge erected.

## PULTENEY BRIDGE.

This elegant structure crosses the Avon from the eastern side of the city; it consists of three lofty arches, and is surmounted on each side by handsome houses, so that no indication of a bridge is perceived by the person who passes over it. Mr. Baldwin succeeded the celebrated Mr. Wood, in projecting new buildings to embellish the city of Bath, and formed immense plans, which have been partly completed. Out of these arose the extensive groups of buildings to which we are conducted, from the central part of the city, by this bridge. The road passes immediately to Great Pulteney-street, beautifully spacious, and uniformly built—to Laura Place—and to Sydney Gardens, the Vauxhall of Bath—to elegant streets, squares, and that huge pile of buildings which covers the greater part of King's Mead Fields and Bathwick Meadows.

PART OF QUEEN SQUARE, BATH.

THE NEW BRIDGE, BATHWICK.

## NEW IRON BRIDGE, BATH.

The present age is distinguished for improvements in all the useful as well as ornamental arts; and iron, from its abundance and comparative cheapness, has been employed for various purposes: hence cylinders, beams, and pumps for steam-engines, boats and barges for canals and navigable rivers, and, lastly, bridges have been constructed of this material.

Iron bridges possess the advantages of lightness, strength, and durability, combined with a superior elegance of form; and as the termination of a great public road, as it enters the precincts of a first-rate city, this erection, in every respect of a superior description, is peculiarly appropriate.

This new road is considerably shorter than the old one through Walcot; it enters the suburb of Bathwick nearly opposite to Sydney Gardens, and the City near its centre, by a second passage over the Avon at Pulteney Bridge.

## QUEEN SQUARE, BATH.

This elegant Square is on the north-west, on high ground, airy, pleasant, and healthy; forming a conspicuous and highly ornamental object from almost every part of the City. It is in length from north to south, between the buildings, three hundred and sixteen feet; and from east to west, the breadth is three hundred and six feet. In the centre there is an enclosure, according to the original design, measuring equally on each side two hundred and six feet: there was originally a reservoir, supplied with clear water from a natural spring; and an obelisk rose from the centre of the reservoir to the height of seventy feet from the foundation; but as, from some cause or other, the spring that supplied the water has been destroyed, or carried off in some other direction, the place has been filled up, and earth raised against the base of the obelisk, by which it has lost ten feet of its altitude, and rises, apparently, baseless, from the ground.

This column was built in 1738, by order of Mr. Nash, in honour of the Prince and Princess of Wales, who had visited Bath about that time.  It bears on its southern side the following inscription :—

In Memory of Honours conferred,
and in Gratitude for Benefits bestowed,
in this City,
By His Royal Highness, FREDERICK, Prince of Wales,
and his
ROYAL CONSORT,
in the year 1738,
This Obelisk is erected
By RICHARD NASH, Esq.

Of the numerous splendid buildings by the celebrated Mr. Wood, the ARCHITECT OF BATH, this of Queen's Square is not the least excellent, and remains a durable monument of his taste and genius.  The statement given by the Architect, of the design and execution of the obelisk, is curious, and accounts for the peculiarity of its terminating in a point.  He observes, that the size of this obelisk is the same as that described by Pliny, which was erected by Ramisses, king of Egypt, about the time of the Trojan war.  " I should not have deviated," he observes, " from the common form of an obelisk, if there had been any other authority for such form than modern examples.  The Egyptian name for this kind of pillar, as Pliny attests, implies a ray of the sun; and, consequently, the pillar that represented such ray, must have terminated, like it, in a point.  It was usual, as Scaliger observes, for the Grecians to make statues of their gods in the form of pyramidal columns, or obelisks, terminating in a point; many of which, the learned Mr. Greaves tells us, he found standing in the East; and from hence I took my authority; in which I shall think myself right, till I am induced to think otherwise, from further information."

The north wing of the Square is composed of stately buildings, so contrived as to give the appearance of a palace, when viewed from a central station.  The body is of the Corinthian order, on a rustic basement, decorated with all the ornaments of that order; and, as the aspect of this pile of building is directly south, it enjoys all the advantages of light and shade from the sun, to give a picturesque appearance, which its situation, raised above the other buildings of the City, insures to it.

The east and west sides are composed of buildings too extensive to bear the character of wings; either of them might, with propriety, form the front for a country villa of the first-rate description.  The houses of the south side form a distinct building; they are of the Ionic order, and nine in number.  The houses facing this Square are all fronted with white freestone, and before each there is an enclosed area, to separate it from the street; the whole may be considered correct as to design, durable as to materials, and beautiful in the execution.

VIEW IN CORN STREET.

BRISTOL.

REDCLIFFE CHURCH, BRISTOL.

LOOKING NORTH.

# THE CHURCH OF ST. MARY REDCLIFF, BRISTOL.

Of this venerable structure, ancient and modern authors have spoken in terms of admiration. Leland characterizes it as " by far the most beautiful of all churches ;" and Camden observes of it, " So large it is, and the workmanship so exquisite, the roof so artificially vaulted with stone, and the tower so high, that in my opinion it is the most elegant of all the parish churches that I have yet seen in England."

This admirable Gothic building was founded in the year 1292, by Simon de Burton, a person distinguished as having been six times elected Mayor of Bristol. The quarries of Dundry supplied the materials ; and having its foundation in a rock of red sandstone, known by the name of Red Cliff, joined to the name of the patron saint to whom it is dedicated, the name is thus appropriated to the church.

In the records of the Mayoralty of Bristol, it is stated, that this building was not completely finished till the year 1364 ; and that even at that early period, the beauty of its architectural embellishments had raised it to celebrity all over England. Its tower and spire were about 250 feet high ; but, in 1445, the spire was nearly destroyed, and the roof of the church much injured, by a violent thunder-storm. The spire has never been rebuilt, but the tower was finished as it now remains, and the whole building completely repaired, by Mr. William Canynge, an opulent merchant, who was several times Mayor of Bristol.

The Church-yard is enclosed by a balustrade of freestone. This Church, though of great extent, has yet a light and airy appearance, from its numerous windows, and tall and slender pillars, with most delicate mouldings. The length of the Church, including the Chapel of our Lady, is 239 feet ; and the cross aisle, 117 feet, from north to south. The breadth of the nave and aisles is 59 feet, and at the transept 44 feet. The body of the Church rises to the height of nearly 60 feet, the roof arched with stone, in the nave and aisles, abounding with beautiful carvings ; the whole covered with lead. A peculiarity in this Church is, in the extension of the aisles through the cross of the transepts.

The principal entrance at the western door is eight feet wide, and twelve feet high ; and there are handsome porches on the northern and southern sides. Three styles of architecture are distinguishable in this building : the oldest is seen in the middle north porch, which, in its pilasters, columns, arches, and mouldings corresponds with the erections of the thirteenth century, and with the time in which Simon de Burton is said to have been engaged in founding, or in re-edifying, a church on this foundation.

The Tower and grand Northern Porch are evidently of a later date than the tracery of the ceilings and the niches ; and mouldings of more elaborate and ornamental workmanship. These are supposed to mark the character of the architecture of the time of Edward III. : the elder William Canynge was member of parliament for Bristol about this time, viz. 1364 and 1384, and probably built these parts of the Church. And though the nave, choir, and transepts are not precisely in the same style, yet the probability must be admitted of their being the work of the same individual. In the door-way entering the vestry, and in Sir Thomas Mede's monument in the north aisle, a more elaborate style of architectural decoration is characteristic of the time it is understood to have been raised— about the year 1430. The tower, richly decorated, the western front, the north transept, and porch of singular appearance, with flying buttresses, pinnacles, and perforated parapets, unite to delight and astonish the beholder. The shelving ground on which this Church is built, necessarily required a numerous flight of steps, by which it is approached on the north; and this circumstance, by adding to the apparent height of the tower, increases its picturesque effect.

## VIEW IN CORN-STREET, BRISTOL.

Many of the most important commercial buildings of the city of Bristol are included in this View. The COUNCIL HOUSE is a new erection on the site of the old building of the same denomination, which was erected in 1703, and pulled down in 1824. The new house is a handsome building of freestone, from the design and under the superintendence of R. Smirke, Esq.: it presents an Ionic front towards Corn-street, which measures 78 feet; and the side towards Broad-street is 68 feet. A figure of Justice, by F. H. Baily, R.A., is placed in a recess in the cornice; over the entrance, and on one side of this figure, is sculptured the royal arms, and on the other the arms of the city; on shields, in relief. The entrance is by a flight of five steps, into the hall, which is 16 feet in width, and in length the whole depth of the building. The ground-floor contains the Mayor's court, with eight offices. The Council Chamber is a noble room, on the upper floor, 38 feet by 22, and 20 feet in height, lighted by a large circular skylight, in the centre: on the same floor, there are two Committee rooms, and four offices. The height of this building is 45 feet: it was finished in 1826.

The EXCHANGE is an elegant structure, built from a plan by Mr. Wood, at an expense of nearly fifty thousand pounds. The north front is of the Corinthian order, upon a rustic basement, extending 110 feet; but the east and west sides are 135 feet each, and it is supposed capable of containing about 1500 persons within its peristyle. The southern front towards the market-place consists of a rustic arcade, which, with its superstructure, forms a central projection supporting a pediment; the tympan of which bears the arms of the city: above this there rises a turret-clock with one face for the Exchange, and another for the Market. The place where the merchants assemble is a peristyle, of capacity sufficient for 1440 persons.

The COMMERCIAL ROOMS, nearly opposite the Exchange, constitute a building erected by the merchants of Bristol, for a public establishment, similar to the Athenæum at Liverpool, or Lloyd's in London. The architect was Mr. C. A. Busby, of London.

CHEDDER CLIFFS, SOMERSETSHIRE.

BROAD STREET, BRISTOL,

FROM THE ARCH-WAY UNDER ST. JOHN'S TOWER.

## BROAD-STREET, BRISTOL.

The entrance to Broad-street is by the original northern gate of the city, under a handsome Gothic arch, supporting the tower belonging to the adjoining parish-church of St. John. On the inside of this gateway are the statues of Belinus and Brennus, the former of whom was the reputed founder of the city, according to the monkish traditions preserved in the writings of Geofrey of Monmouth. These statues of antique appearance have been by some respectable authors believed to be as old as the city; but the more reasonable belief is, that they are coeval with the arch and spire, which were rebuilt in the fourteenth century by Walter Frampton, an opulent merchant, and three times mayor of the city of Bristol.

The Guildhall is a building of considerable antiquity in Broad-street; it has been newly fronted not many years ago. Over the entrance on the southern side is a statue of king Charles II. in a niche; and on the north are the royal arms; both of these are in free-stone, and of superior workmanship. Adjoining the Great Hall, is St. George's Chapel, in which the election of the mayor and sheriffs takes place annually, on the 15th of September. The front of this edifice is 69 feet in extent; and the Great Hall of Justice is in proportion, and lofty; with side galleries; but the accommodations for the professional attendants, are complained of as by no means convenient for the purpose. The Courts of Oyer and Terminer, and of Nisi Prius; the Quarter Sessions, and the Sheriff's Court, as well as the Courts of Conscience and of Requests, are held here; and the meetings to elect the members of Parliament.

## CHEDDER CLIFFS.

These Cliffs, as they rise on each side of the winding valley, present one of the finest pieces of rock-scenery in the kingdom, extending nearly two miles, and being in many places 130 yards high. The village of Chedder overlooks the extensive flat ground and low moors on the south-west, to which this mountainous elevation presents a striking contrast. As we ascend the hill, the first remarkable object is a rapid and clear stream that turns a mill, as it gushes out from the rocks, and flows on towards the river Axe, which it joins at a short distance. As we approach the source of this rivulet, the chasm suddenly presents itself, and strongly attracts our attention; its form and appearance varies as we advance, and seems sometimes to consist of a vast assemblage of rocks, rising behind each other; neither offering to our view any appearance of a passage between or over them. As we proceed, however, we discover that the chasm is continuous, and conducts quite through the whole extent of the south-west ridge of the Mendip, which it divides into two branches, allowing an easy ascent to the top of the hill. In its winding course the path is in a direction nearly from south-west to north-east; the rocks on the right hand rising much higher than on the left, and in some places to the height of 300 feet, frequently presenting singularly picturesque appearances, and bold projecting masses; and where the road is narrowed, the bottom appears covered with huge fragments of broken rocks; and overhead, sapling trees and brushwood, with ivy intermixed, form an impending shade, here and there presenting collections of loosened stones, which seem to threaten destruction to the astonished passenger. In attentively observing the face of the rocks on each side, there appears an exact correspondence in their form and texture, strongly indicating that they have been originally united, and that their dislocation has been effected by the falling down of the lower part of the hill, in some ancient convulsion.

The strata are from one to three feet in thickness, and their inclination nearly toward the south-west; the general direction of the whole mass, being from north-west to south-east. This is the course of these hills, and their height seems to increase northward, particularly near the village of Loxton, where there is a prodigious eminence, called Crook's Peak. These Cliffs have been compared to Dove Dale, in Derbyshire; and, excepting the profusion of wood which covers the latter, there is a resemblance between them; but the scenery of Chedder is on a grander and bolder scale.

Where the passage of the Chedder Cliffs terminates, two roads branch off, and lead to the tops of the hills, which rise several hundreds of feet higher, with a gradual ascent, commanding, to the west and south, the most extensive prospects.

Mendip may properly be termed the Alps of Somersetshire, as the Peak has been of Derbyshire: these immense chains of mountains are exceedingly alike in the natural productions of which they are composed: veins of lead and calamine are distributed throughout both; and in both of them vast caverns and subterraneous vaults are found, and the same species of stone; with the same admixture of coralloid relics in their limestone rocks.

CHEDDER CLIFFS, SOMERSETSHIRE.

LINDRY TOWER, &c. NEAR BRUTON.

## CHEDDER CLIFFS.

### (LOOKING SOUTH.)

These stupendous rocks of Chedder, forming a portion of the Mendip hills, are not only distinguished, as affording sublimely romantic views of great interest to the admirer of nature, but are highly valuable in the inexhaustible treasures which the mineralogist discovers in the strata of which they are formed. These are found to contain rich veins of lead and calamine; copper, magnesia, bole and red-ochre, are also produced, and coal in abundance. In every part of the great range of the Mendip hills, portions of these minerals are found, yet the calcarious formation, denominated the compact gray mountain limestone, constitutes the chief substance of the rocky masses which give rise to all the bold and picturesque scenery so remarkable in this district, and of which the hills of Chedder form the southern extremity.

The river Axe has its source in Chedder cliffs, issuing from the gloomy cavern of Wokey Hole, which is a natural perforation of the rock, in some degree similar to certain excavations in Derbyshire, and like them it is also provided with its witch and its legend.

Several years ago, a dog, thrown into this hole, found his way through the body of the mountain, and came out near the town of Chedder, where a stream issues forth, and which from this occurrence is known to communicate with the cavern, which is more than five miles distant.

Wokey Hole has been noticed by various authors, and particularly in the Philosophical Transactions : by some it is described as about three hundred feet in depth; by others it is said to be unfathomable. It is enclosed by a wall to prevent accidents, fatal to men and beasts. The principal entrance is dangerous to approach, and terrible to behold; a little below this chasm an impending rock is seen, but all beyond is frightful gloom. Visitors throw stones into it, which are heard for some time, dashing against rocks, and at last plunge into water. On the 17th of March, 1775, the Rev. M. Newman, one of the canons of the Cathedral of Bristol, with another gentleman and two ladies, one of them his sister, and the other, the object of his affection, went to explore the depth of this horrible cavity. Mr. N. lowered a line, and being near the dark aperture, in order that he might be safer, laid hold of a part of the root of an ash-tree, which grew over the mouth of it. But his foot slipping, the twig broke, and he was precipitated into this yawning, black, and dreadful gulf, in the sight of his astonished and almost petrified friends. That morning he had officiated at Clifton church, and read the 88th Psalm, in which are these words, strikingly descriptive of his catastrophe : " Thou hast laid me in the lowest pit, in a place of darkness, and in the deep !" After this shocking accident, so many people went from Bristol to view this Hole, that the place about it resembled a fair. Vehicles for descending were contrived, and some went down daily, to search for the body, which was found, thirty-nine days after, floating on the water.

## DUNDRY TOWER.

DUNDRY is the highest hill in this part of the country; its name is derived from the Erse *Dun* and *Draegh*, "The hill of oaks;" with which wood, it was undoubtedly covered in ancient times; and there yet remains some fine groves of oak-trees on its northern side: its western summit has a most bleak and dreary aspect; the cold winds from the channel blow over it; and the stillness of solitude is neither enlivened by the productions of nature, nor the works of art, of which scarcely a vestige appears, excepting a rude building, supposed to have been a beacon-house, of great antiquity; it has two large flat stones inclined against each other to form a roof, and is entered by a low arched door-way. This lofty eminence is fourteen miles distant from Bath, in a westerly direction, and five miles south-west from Bristol, and commands most extensive and beautiful prospects in the west of England. To the north and east the cities of Bath and Bristol are seen; and beyond these to the right, into Wiltshire, the view includes the hills about Calne and Devizes, and the White-horse, at the distance of thirty-five miles. The high ground near Berkley and Stroud in Gloucestershire, are seen beyond Bristol, with the summits of the Malvern hills in Worcestershire. The Severn, as it extends from north to west, is seen to embrace the Welsh coast, and beyond it are the mountains of Wales at a vast distance; as the eye follows the river in its course, the Quantock hills appear, near Bridgwater; and a beautiful and richly cultivated country extends southward, including Stourhead, Knoll Hill, and Clay Hill near Warminster, with the noble plantations of Lord Weymouth and the Duke of Somerset, bounded by the high lands in the vicinity of Shaftesbury.

Dundry church is dedicated to St. Michael the Archangel; it is on a very elevated station, and seen at an immense distance, both by sea and land. It consists of a nave, north aisle, and chancel. A beautiful tower rises from the west-end, ornamented with clustered open turreted pinnacles fifteen feet high above the battlements: there are six bells and a handsome clock; with a staircase leading to the top.

The original building was erected in 1482, but was repaired and enlarged in 1794 at the expense of £1,500. Henry Hellier, a learned divine, and fellow of Corpus Christi College, Oxford, was born in the village of Dundry. He was the author of a sermon, preached before the University of Oxford, and published there in 1687: the subject of this discourse was "the obligation of an oath;" the text being the 4th verse of the 15th Psalm. It was understood to be a bold attack on king James II., impugning him with a breach of his coronation oath. That this feeling prevailed in the neighbourhood, is evident from the following inscription on a brass plate, in the church. "In memory of William and Martha Jones, of Bishport. She died March 3rd 1749, aged 67. He died May 16th 1753, aged 81. He was a man of well-known integrity, and whose natural abilities were so great, that by them only, he clearly comprehended the powers of the human mind; and, unaided by academical education, was able to refute, with uncommon sagacity, the slavish systems of usurped authority over the rights, the consciences, and the reason of mankind"

THE QUAY, ST. AUGUSTINE'S BACK, &c.

BRISTOL.

REDCLIFFE CHURCH & PARADE,

BRISTOL.

BRISTOL, FROM THE AVON.

THE QUAY, WITH THE TOWER OF ST STEPHEN'S.

### BRISTOL, FROM THE AVON—THE QUAY, WITH TOWER OF ST. STEPHEN— ST. AUGUSTINE'S BACK—REDCLIFFE CHURCH, AND PARADE.

The part of the Quay of Bristol named The Back, was formerly of inferior importance; but a canal has been made, which encloses the parishes of St. Mary Redcliffe, and the Temple, nearly in a triangle; its object is to keep a regular supply of water, by the assistance of drains, that vessels may float at low water.

These improvements have been effected at a great expense, and the largest vessels may now proceed to sea from this port, with the lowest neap tides, instead of being compelled to wait for spring tides; sometimes losing weeks, and even months, and the advantages of favouring winds. These beneficial results far exceed the expectations of those by whom the works were originally undertaken. The expense of loading and unloading vessels is considerably diminished, as they now always preserve the same relative position to the walls of the Quay, being no longer elevated or depressed as the tides rise or fall; two navigable rivers have been converted into immense floating docks; and the original warehouses retained and improved, and exceedingly increased in value; and the transactions of commerce rendered more certain, easy, and expeditious. The expense of these works was originally estimated at £300,000, but the actual cost was nearly £600,000.

With these improvements, the Quay of Bristol is one of the finest mercantile havens in Europe; its embankment is a firm solid wall of stone, with large hewn copings, forming one continued wharf of more than a mile in extent, from St. Giles' Bridge to the mouth of the Frome; and up the Avon to Bristol Bridge. Passing along the borders of the City, at various places, the Quay receives peculiar distinguishing names. The original name of Back is retained by the bend of the river from Bristol Bridge to Redcliffe Parade; from whence, following the course of the river, it is called the Grove: in several places there are Docks of considerable extent projecting out from the river, and on one of these, which is on the western side, there is a building on cast-iron pillars, called the Great Crane, used for loading and unloading ships: this curious and importantly useful piece of mechanism, is the workmanship of the ingenious Mr. Padmore; from this place to the mouth of the Frome receives the name of the Gib. The entrance to the Bristol Dock is through St. Giles' Drawbridge, and, by the appointment of the magistrates, officers are stationed here, and paid for attending to admit all vessels on their approach.

On the banks of this river, various conveniences are made for ship-building and repairing; and the Merchants' Floating Dock is of very unusual extent. About two miles lower down the river there is a noble Dock, called Sea Mill Dock, sufficiently capacious to hold 150 vessels.

After passing over the first iron bridge, from the Bath road, we arrive at the **Parade;** which is the nearest and most pleasant road, along the banks of the Avon, to Clifton, and the Hot Wells.   In many places it is beautifully shaded with trees, and in its whole extent is surrounded by interesting objects.   The flight of steps leading to Redcliffe Church rises from the Parade, and, as we proceed along the banks of the river, the retrospect of this venerable structure is exceedingly impressive.

The second iron bridge, of one arch, is at a short distance; and the City Jail, presenting in its construction strength and security.   It is a spacious building, with wings, approached by iron galleries on the highest story.   A high wall surrounds the whole.

Perhaps there is no part of Bristol or its vicinity that presents a more varied or interesting range of scenery than is exhibited before us, as we proceed along this favourite and much-frequented walk; near Brandon Hill Tyndale's Park-house is seen on an eminence; with the Royal and Lower Crescents; Illhouse-dock, with the shipping in the Float; Nova Scotia Wharf, and Cumberland Bason.   In the distance, as we advance, Rawnham Ferry, Watts' Folly, built upon a rock of immense height, and a pleasing view of Dundry Hill, diversify the surrounding prospect.

## ENTRANCE TO BRISTOL—BRIDGE—GENERAL VIEW, &c.

A bridge over the Avon is mentioned by ancient writers as early as the year 1173, which is supposed to have been of wood; and this is probable; for, in 1761, when the old bridge of 1247 was pulled down, the workmen perforated the piers, to discover whether they were strong enough to support the new erection, and found in the middle of Redcliff pier a sill of oak, about a foot square, and forty feet long, with two uprights near each end, about nine inches square, and nine feet high, mortised into it, which they concluded to be the remains of the old wooden bridge, walled up in the pier, to prevent the trouble of taking them out.

The present bridge is constructed of wrought stone, brought from Courtfield, in Monmouthshire; it consists of three wide and lofty arches, with handsome stone balustrades, six feet high; the central arch is elliptical, and the span fifty-five feet, the side arches semicircular, and of forty-feet span.   The piers are in thickness ten feet, and in length forty-two.   There is a raised way for foot-passengers, defended by small iron pillars and chains.   This bridge was opened in 1768.   It is well lighted; and at each end is a toll-house of stone; but, the tolls being discontinued, these are converted into shops.   The river here is deep, and very rapid, and flows to the height of forty feet, so as to bring a vessel of 1000 tons up to the Quay.

GENERAL VIEW OF BRISTOL.

ENTRANCE TO BRISTOL,
FROM THE LONDON ROAD.

GATE-LODGE OF BROOMWELL HOUSE,
BRISLINGTON, NEAR BRISTOL.

COLLEGE GREEN,
BRISTOL.

## COLLEGE GREEN, THE CATHEDRAL, ETC.

The Cathedral of Bristol is dedicated to the Holy and Undivided Trinity, and was originally the collegiate church of the monastery of St. Augustin, founded by Robert Fitzharding, a descendant of the kings of Denmark, and the remote ancestor of the noble family of Berkeley. The monastery itself was destroyed at the period of the dissolution of religious houses by Henry VIII.; and the venerable gateway westward of the cathedral is all that now remains, either to preserve a specimen of its architecture, or to attest its former beauty and magnificence.

The stranger who visits the cathedral should enter it from the cloisters, because by this means he will pass under the interesting specimen of Saxon architecture, which is the present entrance to College Square. The elegance of its finely curved arch, and the richness of its ornaments, cannot fail to excite his admiration; and while he passes under this arch, let him not neglect to observe the pleasing effect produced by the intersections of the circular arches in the walls of each side. It will easily be perceived that these intersections form a pointed arch of the most exact proportions; and it is highly probable that, from observation of the effect thus produced, the pointed architecture of cathedrals derived its origin.

In the Deanery adjoining this arch, resided, for a short period, the celebrated Warburton, who held this preferment from the year 1757, till he obtained a mitre in 1760.

From the cloisters the ascent into the cathedral is to the transept, nearly opposite the south aisle. The approach to the aisles excites an impression of solemn grandeur, produced by the loftiness of the roof. This is said to be the only cathedral in the kingdom in which the centre and side aisles are of equal height.

The choir is mostly occupied by the remains of bishops of the diocese. Near the entrance from the south aisle, three flat stones cover the graves of Bishops Conybeare, Butler, and Bradshaw; the second grave from the entrance being consecrated by the ashes of Dr. Butler.

In the north wall, adjoining the altar, are the tombs of Abbots Knowles and Newbery: the most ancient of these is that nearest the altar, which is erected in an arch over the grave of Abbot Knowles, who died in 1332, and may with great probability be regarded as the builder of the present cathedral. Below is the tomb of Abbot Newbery, who died in 1463; and opposite is a similar tomb, to the memory of Abbot Newland, who died in 1515.

In the aisles are several monuments which deserve attention, not merely for their general style of execution, but also for their inscriptions, which have been admired for an elegance purely classical.

On the left of the transept, entering from the College Green, are steps conducting to the Elder Lady's chapel, in which is the tomb of Fitzharding, the founder of the monastery. Between the steps of this chapel and the entrance, a cross and skull cover the grave of

Abbot Cook, who died in 1366. On the right, against the west wall, are several elegant monuments, of which the first, particularly worthy of notice, is one raised to the memory of Mrs. Elizabeth Draper, the "Eliza" of Sterne. Its form is that of a pointed or gothic arch, within which are two figures, which may be pronounced to be good specimens of the productions of genius in this department of art, for they are in the best manner of their sculptor, Bacon, and will be a lasting testimony of his ability.

## BADMINTON, GLOUCESTERSHIRE.

This magnificent structure, one of the noblest in England, was founded by the princely spirit of one of the house of Somerset, and since the destruction of the ancient family seat at Ragland Castle, in Monmouthshire, which was reduced to bare walls in the time of the Civil War, has ever been the principal residence of the head of the noble family.

The principal front of the Mansion is a stately elevation, constructed in the Palladian style; it is of great extent, and consists of a rustic basement story, in which is the entrance, of the Tuscan order; two columns, rusticated on the shafts, support a corresponding entablature and pediment. The centre division of the building has an air of much grandeur, and is adorned by a colonnade of the Composite order, surmounted by an attic; in a pediment, is a circular cartouche shield sculptured with the arms of Somerset, ducally crowned, which are, *Quarterly, France and England, within a border, componé*, his Grace deriving his descent from a branch of the house of Plantagenet. The wings, which extend considerably upon each side, are designed with more simplicity, and give a noble effect to the architectural elevation, which is terminated by Tuscan archways to the Stables and Offices. Over each extremity of the centre is a cupola and vane. In the distant view from the Park, the Mansion is seen to the fullest advantage; the scenery around, though neither grand nor romantic, is of the most pleasing character, greatly aiding the magnificent appearance of the building. Internally this seat is splendid in its decorations; the rooms are spacious and elegantly ornamented. In the Great Dining-room is a profusion of admirable carving in wood, by Grinlin Gibbons; and in the Picture Gallery, a fine series of Family Portraits; a portrait of William Shippen, the satirical poet; and a curious representation of the different Sovereigns of Europe by various animals, painted by Salvator Rosa.

The Park is very extensive, being above nine miles in circumference. It is of an oblong form, about three miles long and nearly two miles wide, situated in the Hundred of Grymbald's Ash, about five miles east from Sodbury, and bordering upon Wiltshire, on the west, about seven miles from Malmsbury. It contains some very fine woods and beautiful drives. The parish church, which formerly belonged to the Abbey of Pershore, was rebuilt at the expense of the late Duke of Beaufort, in the year 1785. It stands within the Park, a little south-east of the Mansion; its tower with pinnacles is seen rising over the house.

BADMINTON,
(GENERAL VIEW)
GLOUCESTERSHIRE

Drawn by J.P.Neale.                    Engraved by W. Radclyffe.

BADMINTON,
GLOUCESTERSHIRE

WELLS CATHEDRAL.

WHINGTON CHURCH.

## WRINGTON CHURCH.

This is an admired and stately edifice, consisting of a nave, chancel, aisles, and a porch with richly ornamented pinnacles. The tower is 160 feet high, with battlements and turrets. At the terminating point of the roof is a small elegant turret, surmounted by a cross, with an opening below, intended for the bell to call to morning and evening prayers. The columns of the arches of the nave, which is lofty, are clustered, the exterior being continued up to the moulding of the windows, and then terminating in figures bearing shields. The chancel is separated from the corresponding end of the side aisle, by an oak screen of light and curious workmanship. Old reading-desks are still remaining, fastened to the walls of the chancel, on which are copies of several works of some antiquity.

## WELLS CATHEDRAL.

This cathedral erected in 1239, by bishop Joceline de Wells, is esteemed one of the most superb pieces of Gothic architecture in the kingdom; it is situated at the east end of the city, and is built in the form of a cross, being in length from east to west three hundred and eighty feet, and from north to south one hundred and eighty feet: this structure contains nine chapels, one of which, dedicated to the Virgin, is highly admired for its beautiful and delicate Gothic windows: in the centre of the transepts, is a large handsome quadrangular tower, resting on four fine arches, and containing five bells: the west front is flanked by two smaller towers, in the south-west of which is a ring of eight very large bells; this front is allowed to be remarkably fine and imposing, being covered with a profusion of statues, beautifully sculptured, in niches or recesses, the vaults of which are supported by elegant slender pillars of polished Purbeck marble; at the top are the Apostles, below them are the Hierarchs; and one whole line, of the breadth of the portal, is occupied by a grotesque representation of the Resurrection: the interior of the whole cathedral is richly decorated, and the great west window contains some ancient painted glass: besides many tombs and monuments of bishops and eminent men, there is a large stone in the centre of the nave, ascribed to king Ina, the original founder; the cloister of the cathedral is esteemed a fine building, and the chapter-house is of an octagonal form, having its roof supported by a fine clustered pillar of Purbeck marble. The chief curiosity is Peter Lightfoot's clock, standing in an old chapel of the north transept, brought hither from Glastonbury, and is a most singular piece of mechanism, for the age in which it was invented.

## VIEW OF WELLS.

This city (jointly with Bath, the see of a bishop) is situated at the south foot of the Mendip hills, near the source of the river Axe, and consists of several parallel streets, intersected by smaller ones. In general they are well built and neatly paved, and the market-place is wide and airy. The principal public buildings are—the market-house, erected in the room of its ancient and curious cross; the town-hall, in which the assizes are holden alternately with Bridgewater and Taunton, and the public business transacted; the parish church of St. Cuthbert; and the magnificent cathedral already described.

## VIEW OF GLOUCESTER.

This city, the see of a bishop, is situated in the Vale of Gloucester, on a gentle eminence, rising on the east side from the river Severn. Very considerable improvements in its appearance and buildings have been recently made, the streets being now well paved and lighted, and various edifices and projections, obstructing the free passage of carriages, having been removed: formerly the houses were chiefly of timber, which at several periods occasioned the destruction of a large proportion of the city by accidental fires; they are now principally of brick. From the intersection of the four chief streets, the buildings occupy an easy descent each way; a circumstance which greatly contributes to health and cleanliness; and it is supplied with water from springs in the neighbourhood. In the city and suburbs of Gloucester were formerly eleven parochial churches, besides the cathedral, many of which are not now standing. The buildings most worthy of notice, are,—the cathedral; the county infirmary; the county goal and penitentiary, constructed on Mr. Howard's plan; and the house of industry: the walls which formerly surrounded the city, were completely demolished soon after the Restoration; and the only memorial of the former strength of the fortification left remaining was the west gate, standing on the banks of the Severn, at the end of a stone bridge over that river. This city was anciently regarded as a distinct hundred, and it is still privileged as a county within itself. The Severn is navigable to the wharf near the bridge for small vessels, but those of more considerable burden can only get up at spring tides, the narrow channel of the river near the city being obstructed by rocks and sandbanks: to remedy this inconvenience, the Gloucester canal was projected. The schools and charitable institutions are numerous, and conducted on such liberal principles as do credit to the inhabitants. The honour of founding this city is due to the Britons: its neighbourhood was frequently the scene of action between them and the Saxons, and the early importance of the place is evinced by its having been the residence of several Saxon monarchs. During the civils wars, the inhabitants sided with the Parliament; and their opposition to their king is very generally supposed to have operated fatally against that unfortunate monarch's interest in the kingdom. On this account the walls were demolished at the Restoration.

WELLS,

SOMERSETSHIRE.

GLOUCESTER,

FROM ROBIN'S WOOD HILL.

COTHELSTONE HOUSE.

SOMERSETSHIRE.

SANDHILL PARK.

SOMERSETSHIRE.

## COTHELSTONE HOUSE, SOMERSETSHIRE,

The seat of Edward Jeffries Esdaile, Esq., stands in the parish of Bishop's Lydiard, within the hundred of Kingsbury West, seven miles north-west from Taunton. The Mansion, erected a few years back by the present proprietor, affords as correct and chaste a specimen of the Grecian Ionic architecture, as the nature of our domestic buildings will allow. The south or principal front (see our View) has coupled pilasters supporting a regular entablature throughout; the centre being broken by two columns, which, with the capitals, mouldings, cornice, &c., are taken from the temple of *Minerva Polias* at Athens. The house is built of white sandstone from a quarry recently discovered on the estate. The ornaments of the interior are in character with those already described. The stair-case is in good taste, the light to which from the roof is admitted by a circular horizontal window of stained glass, in a frame of cast bronze, over which is a skylight. The house is not large, being only seventy-four feet by sixty-eight. The offices are connected by a back wing, concealed by plantations. The situation of Cothelstone House yields to none in the county in natural beauties and advantages. The vale of Taunton lies to the south, backed by the Brown-down and Blackdown Hills, from an opening in which, Halsdown by Exeter, thirty miles distant, is visible. An ancient round tower, called the Lodge, and which is taken advantage of as a landmark by ships in the British channel, affords a very extensive prospect, offering to the eye, on a clear day, and with the aid of a good glass, a sight of fourteen counties. From hence the line of the Quantock Hills runs to the north-west, terminating at the ocean; they are mostly covered with heath and wortleberry. The black cock is found in considerable numbers, and the eagle has been occasionally seen : a specimen of one lately killed is in the Institution at Taunton.

## SANDHILL PARK, SOMERSETSHIRE.

Sandhill Park, the seat of Sir Thomas Buckler Lethbridge, Bart., M.P., is a beautiful wooded spot, commanding magnificent views of the vale bounded by the Quantock Hills on the north-east, and the Black-down Hills to the south; it is situated partly in the parish of Bishop's Lydiard, and partly in the parish of Ash Priors, in the hundred of Kingsbury West, and contiguous to Taunton Dean, Somersetshire; and has been now in the possession of Sir Thomas Lethbridge, his father Sir John Lethbridge, and his great uncle, the late John Periam, Esq., from the building of the Mansion about the year 1720; since which it has undergone, at different times, many improvements, particularly in the year 1815, when it was inherited by the present owner, who then added two wings to the main body of the house, containing several apartments of large dimensions: among others a library, fifty feet by twenty-six; and a dining-room, fifty by thirty. In the library there is a good collection of books, both ancient and modern; and in the great hall of entrance, the stair-case, and drawing-room, are many valuable pictures.

## KING-WESTON, SOMERSETSHIRE.

The mansion of King-Weston, the seat of William Dickinson, Esq., M.P., is built of fine grey-stone, found on the estate. The interior is divided into many commodious and elegant apartments, containing a choice collection of pictures, and some very fine Italian bronzes, copies of the best Greek statues; and also of the statues of the 15th century now at Rome and Florence. The View presented in the accompanying Plate, shews the two principal fronts, and was sketched from the gardens. The carriage front is ornamented with an elegant portico of the Doric order, recently executed by W. Wilkins, Esq. The village of King-Weston is finely situated, twelve miles south from Wells. Most of the houses are built of blue stone, and are in general very neat. This place is memorable for a signal defeat, which the rebels of Devonshire and Cornwall experienced in the third year of the reign of Edward VI. The church is a small neat building, situated on the highest part of the parish, surrounded with lofty elms and chesnut trees. It has an embattled tower, containing a clock and three bells. Against the north wall of the chancel in an elegant monument of black and white marble, with this inscription :—" M. S. Caleb Dickinson hic sepulti, qui obiit 6$^{to.}$ Aprilis 1783; et Saræ uxoris, apud Bristoliam sepultæ, quæ obiit 1$^{mo.}$ Julii 1766. Posuit Gulielmus filius, Anno 1783.—Arms :—*Or, a bend engrailed, between two Lions rampant, gules.* The Living is a Rectory in the Deanery of Cary. William Dickinson, Esq., the present Lord of the Manor of King-Weston, has for many years represented the county of Somerset in Parliament.

## ENMORE CASTLE, SOMERSETSHIRE.

The situation of Enmore Castle, the seat of the Right Hon. John Perceval, Earl of Egmont, is on a gently rising ground in the midst of a fine enclosed country, about five miles from Bridgewater, and eight from Taunton. The present Mansion-house was built by John Perceval, first Earl of Egmont, on the spot where formerly stood the old family residence of the Malets. It is a large quadrangular embattled pile, constructed of a dark reddish-coloured stone, flanked at each angle by a low square machiolated tower; with bastion and two circular towers and drawbridge at the principal entrance leading to a spacious court-yard, (See the annexed Engraving.) The offices are under ground, and look out upon a dry fosse, forty feet wide, and sixteen feet deep, which surrounds the Castle : on the opposite side of the fosse are the stables and out-houses. The interior of the Castle is splendidly fitted up, and contains many family portraits, and, among other objects of interest, the bed on which the late Queen Caroline expired.—His late Majesty, George III., was pleased, in May, 1762, to bestow upon John, second Earl of Egmont, the dignity of a Peer of Great Britain, by the title of Lord Lovell and Holland, Baron of Enmore, in the county of Somerset. The late Right Hon. Spencer Perceval, Chancellor of the Exchequer, who was assassinated, was a son of John, second Earl of Egmont, brother to the late. and uncle to the present Earl.—Motto : *Sub cruce candida.*

**KING-WESTON,**

SOMERSETSHIRE.

**ENMORE CASTLE,**

SOMERSETSHIRE.

CIRENCESTER PARK.
GLOUCESTERSHIRE.

BATSFORD.
GLOUCESTERSHIRE.

## CIRENCESTER PARK, GLOUCESTERSHIRE.

This large and noble mansion, the seat of Earl Bathurst, adjoins the town of Cirencester, which is situated on the little river Churn.    The park and grounds are very extensive, and abound with fine woods and avenues; ten of the latter meet in a centre, of which
three are some miles long, one nearly five miles in length: this avenue runs east and west;
at the eastern extremity the tower of Cirencester Church is seen to great advantage.    On
leaving the woods and avenues, which are much dressed in their appearance, a very
different scenery presents itself; another park, called Pinbury Park, by the removal of
roads and fences, has been united, and brought into one domain : the grounds here are
wild and romantic, with large trees on the rugged sides of the hills; a long valley unites
itself with Sapperton Vale, and extensive drives and rides have been lately made, con-
trasting greatly with the formal avenues, no longer visible.    The west front of the Mansion, of which we have given the view, consists of a centre, surmounted by an elliptical
pediment, with a range of building on either side; modern additions upon the north have
extended this front to a great length.    Cirencester Church rises above the buildings.    The
House now opens to a beautiful lawn, backed by a wooded scenery of the most luxurious
description, Oakley park and woods being connected with the grounds at this point; and
about a mile from the house, nearly in the centre of the Deer park, stands a lofty column
bearing a colossal statue of Queen Anne : there is also a fine terrace, adorned with buildings, and flanked by plantations of shrubs and evergreens.

In the Entrance Hall is a very fine equestrian portrait of the Duke of Wellington, by
Sir Thomas Lawrence.    The Duke is represented in the actual dress worn by him during
the whole of the day of the battle of Waterloo; every article of which he put on to sit
for this picture, and the very horse he rode on that important day, named Copenhagen,
was taken to Sir Thomas Lawrence, that the likeness might be complete.

## BATSFORD PARK, GLOUCESTERSHIRE.

This mansion, the seat of Lord Redesdale, is situated on a declivity of the Coteswold
Hills, six miles north from Stow in the Wold, and about a mile and a half from Moreton
in Marsh, in the direct road from London to Worcester.    The House is constructed of
stone, with considerable attention to architectural propriety; on the entrance front is a
Doric portico.    Our view, from the meadow below the terrace wall of the gardens, shows
more particularly the south side, where the House appears to great advantage, backed by
noble woods : it is not more than two stories in height, and is surmounted with bold
blocked cornice and balustraded parapet.    The grounds possess a variety of natural beauties, improved by art.    The ancient name of this place was Becsore, or Bechesore ; probably derived from a pointed hill, the extremity of the Coteswold, distinguished by some
old beech trees : " ore" signifying a point of land.

## SEZINCOT, GLOUCESTERSHIRE.

This elegant mansion, the seat of Sir Charles Cockeril, Bart., is seated about two miles and a half from the town of Morton, about seven from Camden, and nineteen miles north-east from the city of Gloucester. It has been entirely erected by the present owner of the estate, and in the style of the splendid palaces of the East. The grounds are varied and beautiful, and the whole laid out with very great taste and judgment; a part is called the Thornery. These have been embellished with a variety of ornamental buildings erected in the most picturesque situations. The Wellington Pillar, the Temple, the Bridge, and Fountain, are subjects of the pencil of Thomas Daniell, Esq. R.A., an artist well known for his exquisite delineations of Oriental scenery: his paintings of the views at Sezincot were exhibited at Somerset House, in the year 1819.

## ADLESTROP PARK, GLOUCESTERSHIRE.

Adlestrop is a large and interesting mansion, the seat of Chandos Leigh, Esq.: a portion of it appears of considerable antiquity, to which additions have been made in later times. It is delightfully situated on the gentle slope of a hill near the boundary of the county, where it adjoins Oxfordshire, about four miles north-east from the town of Stow in the Wold. The pleasure-grounds by which it is environed, were laid out by the late Adey Repton, who has not failed to display the natural beauties of the situation to the greatest advantage. A small stream, which rushes down a declivity over a rocky bed, falls into a lake at some distance from the house. The parish is bounded on the west by the river Evenlode, which flows into the Isis. The name is supposed by Atkyns to be derived from the Saxon *Ædle*, noble, and *Throp*, habitation. The manor and estate belonged to the Abbey of Evesham from the Conquest to its dissolution; after which, in the seventh of Edward VI., it was granted to Sir Thomas Leigh, Knt., a member of a very ancient family of that name in Cheshire, who was Lord Mayor of London in the first year of Queen Elizabeth's reign, and left at his decease, in the fourteenth year of her reign, three sons, Rowland, Thomas, and William, and assigned his estate at Adlestrop to the eldest, which has remained the seat and residence of the representative of the eldest branch of the family, until they inherited Stoneleigh Abbey, in Warwickshire, their principal estate, which had been bequeathed in the reign of Elizabeth to Thomas, the second son of Sir Thomas Leigh, Knt.

SESINCOT.

GLOUCESTERSHIRE

ADLESTROP.

GLOUCESTERSHIRE.

LEIGH COURT, THE MOUTH OF THE AVON.
WITH DISTANT VIEW OF THE WELSH COAST

CLIFTON.

## CLIFTON,

Is charmingly situated on the summit of the northern cliffs, immediately above the river Avon, about two miles from Bristol. It has been justly celebrated for the natural beauties of its situation, although little advantage has been taken of this by art, many of the buildings being ill-constructed, and so arranged as to intercept the view of each other. The vicinity, however, is fine; and Clifton, in the spring of the year, is numerously attended, both by people of fashion and invalids: its hot-spring has long been renowned; and its air is so pure and salubrious, as to occasion its being styled the Montpellier of England. The numerous lodging-houses, hotels, public libraries, &c., with which this village is surrounded, are elegant, commodious, and comfortable. From Clifton Down are the most beautiful prospects; and the remains of fortifications, entrenchments, &c., prove it to have been a Roman station. A suspension bridge across the Avon, from cliff to cliff, is intended to be constructed; which will not only prove of vast advantage in facilitating the landing of passengers by the steam-packets, &c., but will form one of the most extraordinary objects of art: it may even be expected to rival, if not to exceed, the celebrated Menai suspension bridge, at present esteemed the greatest achievement of the kind in the united kingdom.

## LEIGH COURT, &c.

This subject well deserves the pencil of a Claude: the scenery is luxuriant, and the prospects delightfully varied; in the distance, the Bristol channel is seen, with the Welsh coast beyond. The south or principal entrance to this noble Mansion, (commenced by P. J. Miles, Esq. in 1814,) has an Ionic portico; on the north front is a similar one, and to the east a colonnade. The principal apartments are—a Vestibule on the south side; on the left a Billiard-room, and Study; on the opposite side a Music-room, which leads into the Library; and beyond this is the Drawing-room, which opens into the Saloon; on the other side of which is the Dining-room. In the centre of the building is the Great Hall, with which all the apartments on the principal story communicate. The Staircase leads to an open Gallery, in connexion with the sleeping apartments, which occupy the first story. The rooms are elegantly furnished, and contain an extensive collection of Paintings, mostly by foreign artists of eminence: many of them originally adorned the palaces of Italy, previous to its invasion by the French army, during the consular dynasty.

The Arms